Becoming a Software Company

Accelerating Business Success through Software

Amarinder Sidhu

Apress®

Becoming a Software Company: Accelerating Business Success through Software

Amarinder Sidhu
Bay Area, CA, USA

ISBN-13 (pbk): 978-1-4842-9168-9 ISBN-13 (electronic): 978-1-4842-9169-6
https://doi.org/10.1007/978-1-4842-9169-6

Managing Director, Apress Media LLC: Welmoed Spahr
Acquisitions Editor: Shiva Ramachandran
Development Editor: James Markham
Coordinating Editor: Jessica Vakili

Distributed to the book trade worldwide by Springer Science+Business Media New York, 1 New York Plaza, New York, NY 10004. Phone 1-800-SPRINGER, fax (201) 348-4505, e-mail orders-ny@springer-sbm.com, or visit www.springeronline.com. Apress Media, LLC is a California LLC and the sole member (owner) is Springer Science + Business Media Finance Inc (SSBM Finance Inc). SSBM Finance Inc is a **Delaware** corporation.

For information on translations, please e-mail booktranslations@springernature.com; for reprint, paperback, or audio rights, please e-mail bookpermissions@springernature.com.

Apress titles may be purchased in bulk for academic, corporate, or promotional use. eBook versions and licenses are also available for most titles. For more information, reference our Print and eBook Bulk Sales web page at http://www.apress.com/bulk-sales.

Printed on acid-free paper

Table of Contents

About the Author

Amarinder Sidhu is a Managing Director at Deloitte. He has two decades of hands-on experience in all aspects of enterprise software: business strategy, technology implementations, product management, and software engineering. As an executive, he focuses on building high growth enterprise software products and effective team-based software engineering operations.

Amarinder has an MBA from University of California, Irvine, and an engineering degree from Thapar University, Patiala, India.

https://www.linkedin.com/in/amarindersidhu/
https://twitter.com/amarsidhu

Introduction

"You may not know in your mind where you are going, but you know it by doing"

—Nassim Nicholas Taleb

I don't want to go, I thought.

My client was requesting me to speak to his global IT team about "high-quality product software development, management, and ownership". He wanted me to do a half-day workshop on how internal IT teams should think, behave and operate like a software company.

A few months earlier, during the sales cycle, this client had visited our product headquarters in Boston and quizzed us on all aspects of our team operations in a day-long conversation. He was validating if we knew how to think, behave, and operate like a software company. At that time, my team and I impressed him enough that he was now asking me to share the same perspective with his team.

I was reluctant because everything we were doing or had done was in the context of our operations. In no way did I consider myself a general expert on software engineering, product management, or software development operations. I was concerned if I had enough to say to hold the attention of 20 people for half a day.

However, this was an important client. It took some cajoling from my seniors, but I agreed to go. The first problem was I didn't have a comprehensive slide deck which was worrying a few on our account team. Even they thought that I would run out of things to say. But having been in software product development for the last six years, I had come to detest making slides the way consultants do. So, I decided that I would only talk about things I have done or knew deeply from my experience. I wouldn't present myself as an expert, or as a consultant, but speak from my heart, from my experience as an engineer, a manager, an executive. Despite that resolution, I was proceeding with trepidation. But it turned out to be the best approach to take.

During the session, I realized that I have a lot to say. I shared a few lessons from my experience, then listened and answered questions. A candid and wide-ranging conversation on challenges in enterprise software followed: how to manage business and IT relationships, how to create product roadmaps with ever-changing business requirements, how to become agile when everything around you isn't, how to build product teams, how to manage software talent within the enterprise. I didn't have all the answers but everyone, including me, walked away from the conversation better equipped to find the answers. The conversation helped me to organize these challenges under the framework of *becoming a software company* for the first time.

These were some of the same challenges I was facing, and continue to face, while building enterprise software products within a firm that is not a software company.

I always find it interesting how when a particular worldview (*becoming a software company*) comes into your focus, you start noticing the problem pattern elsewhere. I observed it at many other enterprise clients struggling with the efficiency of their software programs. More broadly, I saw it in the struggle of car manufacturers grappling with challenges of shipping software, health enterprises trying to launch health and medical software, institutions creating virtual experiences to cope with the pandemic.

Even before the pandemic hit, we knew that software, when done right, can create infinite business leverage. It is no coincidence that 8 out of 10 largest companies in the world are software companies[1]. Due to these software companies' "winner takes all" financial success and the potential of software, there was this call to action, shrill and persistent, reverberating in boardrooms, earnings calls, and technology conferences:

Every company should be a software company.

While the call makes rhetorical sense, *becoming a software company* is much harder in a practical sense. There is no formal knowledge. The educational curriculums teach computer science, not how to build good software. The best know-how about building software is practical wisdom amongst the best engineers. And the software management expertise honed by these dominant software-first companies hasn't propagated outside. Beyond this small segment of companies and Silicon Valley-driven software ecosystem, the enterprises like my client are grappling with how to *become a software company.*

Billion-dollar companies are unable to build essential consumer experience apps[2]. GE Digital wanted to be a "top 10 software company" by 2020[3]. Yet, it has struggled to develop its flagship software platform despite spending billions of dollars[4]. WhatsApp had only 50 or so employees when Facebook bought it for $19B. But I see similar-sized teams spin wheels on enterprise software projects of a few million dollars as a matter of routine. It turns out *software eats the world*[5], but only on the consumer software side, not on the enterprise side. The software-driven future that Marc Andreessen predicted in his now-famous 2011 "software is eating the world" essay is here but unevenly distributed. With this book, I am making an attempt to smoothen out this unevenness.

But first, we need to draw a finer boundary around where this challenge lies. For as long as I have been in the software industry, enterprise and consumer software have existed on different planets, and nobody cared. That was just how it was or meant to be.

Enterprise software enables enterprises to run their internal operation. It is a world of specialized databases for various lines of business: Sales, Marketing, Service, HR, Finance, ERP, etc. Because the users were captive, i.e., enterprise employees, there is little to no emphasis on user experience. It evolves slower–*"why fix it if ain't broke"* taken to an extreme conclusion.

On the other hand, consumer software goes into the hands of the consumers–think Google Search, Uber, Amazon.com, Facebook, Instagram, TikTok. And in contrast to the enterprise software, it is perceived as cool. It is user-friendly (maybe too friendly!). It evolves very fast. These software-first companies are magnets for software engineering talent and have unparalleled software operations.

But in "software eats the world" reality, the boundary between enterprise and consumer software is disappearing. IEEE reports that 40% of the cost of a new car comes from software[6]. Elsewhere, software is becoming synonymous with medical devices and therapeutics[7]. The much celebrated trends of FinTech and EdTech are primarily about personalization through cloud scale software deployed through mobile platforms. In this new reality, *becoming a software company* means enterprises have to learn how to ship good and innovative customer-facing software. How? Not an easy question to answer. I am writing this book to provide a possible answer.

There is no shortage of software advice. Why bother writing a book on such a crowded topic?

One can almost point at the cottage industries around all individual facets of software: Design, Product, Agile, DevOps. To me, all these facets are just tactics. I want to draw a holistic connection across these for *building* great software. This advice is also heavy on methods and doesn't explore the fundamental principles. As a result, the methodologies become an end in themselves rather than a means to an end. The search for methodological silver bullets has prompted a software world's very own irrational exuberance — a widespread cargo-culting of technology and best practice adoption that leads nowhere.

Even with very capable software technologies, there is no silver bullet. So I want to outline a practical roadmap for the enterprises tired of cargo-culting, and the accompanied financial drain. I will be compiling the timeless principles on *building* good software, and *building* in general, known before and since the advent of software, but applied in the organizational context of the enterprises. The principles that I see and have seen getting violated while building and deploying enterprise software for the last 17 years.

I will be drawing on my general work experience as an enterprise software practitioner for the last 18 years, first as a software delivery consultant and then as a software product developer. While progressing from a Consultant to a Managing Director, I have engaged with enterprise software practitioners at all levels, including executives. Thus, my expertise enables me to share specific and actionable perspectives for all my readers.

Despite the widespread *"every software company should be software company"* narrative, we are still in the very early stages of the software revolution. While we see the economic impact software technologies can create, we are still grasping at straws for understanding the organizational imperatives of deploying software revolution broadly. The promised information golden age that everyone wants to get in a hurry will only happen if we deploy software the right way in the enterprise. The software revolution that has created immense value within consumer software, and for sellers of enterprise software, needs to propagate to the enterprises.

It is said, *history doesn't repeat but rhymes.* In order to solve our current predicament of creating the missing value with software in enterprise requires listening to the rhymes from the history of technological revolutions. They teach us that we will only make progress by understanding software not as incremental digital transformation technology but as a new paradigm of business innovation.

References

[1] *Biggest companies in the world by market cap 2022.* (2022, August 5). Statista. Retrieved August 15, 2022, from https://www.statista.com/statistics/263264/top-companies-in-the-world-by-market-capitalization/

[2] Belden, J. (2020, March 10). *Lessons from the Hertz vs. Accenture Transformation Disaster.* UpperEdge. Retrieved July 28, 2022, from https://upperedge.com/erp-program-management/4-lessons-from-the-hertz-vs-accenture-disaster/

[3] Dignan, L. (2015, September 14). *GE forms GE Digital, aims to be top 10 software company.* ZDNet. Retrieved July 15, 2022, from https://www.zdnet.com/article/ge-forms-ge-digital-aims-to-be-top-10-software-company/

[4] Mann, T., & Gryta, T. (2020). *Lights Out: Pride, Delusion, and the Fall of General Electric.* Houghton Mifflin Harcourt.

[5] Andreessen, M. (2011, August 20). *Why Software Is Eating the World.* Andreessen Horowitz. Retrieved May 5, 2022, from https://a16z.com/2011/08/20/why-software-is-eating-the-world/

[6] Charette, R. N. (2021, June 7). *How Software Is Eating the Car.* https://spectrum.ieee.org/. Retrieved June 1, 2022, from https://spectrum.ieee.org/software-eating-car

[7] *Software as a Medical Device (SaMD).* (2018, December 4). US FDA. Retrieved June 5, 2022, from https://www.fda.gov/medical-devices/digital-health-center-excellence/software-medical-device-samd

PART 1

Understanding Software as a Medium of Producing Value

As an enterprise, understand how you can leverage software as a value-creating paradigm as described in the following principles.

CHAPTER 1

Don't Pursue Transformations; Make the Software Shift

The Shift Principle

> *Something momentous happened around the year 2000: a major new soft technology came of age. After written language and money, software is only the third major soft technology to appear in human civilization. Fifteen years into the age of software, we are still struggling to understand exactly what has happened. Marc Andreessen's now-familiar line, software is eating the world, hints at the significance, but we are only just beginning to figure out how to think about the world in which we find ourselves.*
>
> —*Venkatesh Rao*

© Amarinder Sidhu 2023
A. Sidhu, *Becoming a Software Company*, https://doi.org/10.1007/978-1-4842-9169-6_1

> *A technological revolution can more generally be defined as a major upheaval of the wealth-creating potential of the economy, opening a vast innovation opportunity space and providing a new set of associated generic technologies, infrastructures and organisational principles that can significantly increase the efficiency and effectiveness of all industries and activities.*
>
> —*Carlota Perez*

The need for *digital transformation* is driving enterprise software for the last decade and a half now. It is an idea that has warmed the hearts of millions in the industry and launched countless software sales and enterprise implementation programs.

But for the enterprise companies, *digital transformation* isn't translating into *business transformation.* In 2016, Forbes estimated the risk of failure for digital transformations at 84%.[1] The more recent analyses, depending on who you ask, put that risk anywhere between 70% and 95%.[2][3][4] Even if you discount the typical hyperbole of business media, these numbers are startling.

Enterprise companies don't get real business transformation. Instead, they get saddled with new and expensive software subscriptions every year. Similar to a hamster running on a wheel, they spend money for whatever trend the transformation zeitgeist calls for: cloud computing, big data, SaaS (Software as a Service), digital customer, Agile product development, DevOps, and Generative-AI. I will only name a few of the trends because the list is long.

This ever-changing zeitgeist has made selling packaged enterprise software the best business there is. Across the continuum of enterprise software, there are big vendors like AWS, Microsoft, and Google. Behind them, many others have found new ways of solving old enterprise problems on the cloud, for example, Salesforce, Workday, NetSuite, Marketo, Snowflake, and Twilio. Beyond them, hundreds of others are monetizing small templates of enterprise business workflows with software.

Currently, enterprise software is a fast-growing $600+billion industry.[5] The market revenues have doubled between 2009 and 2019, which roughly coincides with enterprises embracing cloud based software. Such has been the excitement with the power of new software technologies. *Digital* has become the default representation of solutions for every old and new business problem. And the promise of *transformation* is all you need to sell a technology whether or not there is a valuable business use case. These two words have become *suitcase words*.[6] They represent a suitcase of ideas but hold no specific meaning by themselves.

And it doesn't matter where an entity sits in the enterprise software industry. Whether it is a software seller, a software service provider, or an enterprise, everyone is marching to the drumbeat of *digital transformation*. The COVID-19 crisis pushed this beat to a crescendo. Now, the phenomenon gets invoked as a secular trend driving the business change. When the pandemic forced an accelerated adoption of its Teams software, Microsoft's CEO Satya Nadella remarked on an earnings call[7]: "We've seen two years' worth of digital transformation in two months." Feeling happy about Salesforce's growth during the pandemic, CEO Marc Benioff believes digital transformation is a "must-have."[8] Andy Jassy, previously chief of AWS and now CEO-elect of Amazon, thinks enterprises "looking for transformation want their applications engineered for the cloud."[9]

It seems *digital transformation* has become everyone's cause. But the required effect of *business transformation* doesn't get discussed enough.

What Satya, Marc, and Andy are selling is transformational, but for their companies. For their buyers, i.e., the enterprise companies, there is only potential with what is available to solve their unique business problems. The real opportunity lies beyond the mere adoption of these new technologies for existing ways of doing business.

How Software Ate the Enterprise (IT Stack)

There have been three broad eras of enterprise software.

In the beginning, there was an era of *digitization*. It represented a shift from paper-based records to digital records. The state of the art was a well-performing database with an interface to manage records. This era was headlined by the leading providers of enterprise database software, for example, IBM, Oracle, and Microsoft.

Digitized workflows created a logical question: can you use the data from digitized records to simplify the work within an enterprise? That triggered the era of *digitalization*. I remember when I was starting my career in 2003, every decent-sized enterprise was building data warehouses and implementing business intelligence tools. Enterprises were reimagining their business workflows based on the operational insights from the data. IBM, Oracle, and Microsoft continued to be the leading vendors of enterprise software.

Digitization and *digitalization* were IT-only trends. That is, the software was used to run internal operations. In 2003, and for a few years after, we were largely working on business transformations of the digitization and digitalization variety. Then somewhere around the early 2010s, we started calling those transformations as digital transformations. It coincided with "software eating the world" phenomena getting traction within the enterprise.

Cloud computing unlocked newer ways to build and deliver software. Whether it was Software as a Service (SaaS), Infrastructure as a Service (IaaS), or Platform as a Service (PaaS), a part of the IT stack was "eaten" by software services accessible via the Internet (see Figure 1-1). I call this the *XaaS* era of enterprise software—where X stands for infrastructure, platform, software, or some mix. XaaS software *ate* the enterprise IT stack and pulled the enterprises into the age of software.

With that, there are a lot more building blocks for enterprise applications, which makes a lot more possible for the enterprise companies to do with software. The same machine learning API that Google uses for voice recognition is now available to the enterprise to transcribe the call center phone calls. If an enterprise likes, they can build on Twilio's suite of APIs to build world-class cloud-based contact centers. There are SaaS options available for every line of enterprise business, if they want to avoid building.

However, this type of flexibility is not an unalloyed good. It creates two new challenges for the enterprise companies. First, they increase the *complexity* of the infrastructure required for designing, building, and shipping software applications. Second, everyone uses the same building blocks which necessitates extra work for *differentiation* of the actual software solution that has to be built.

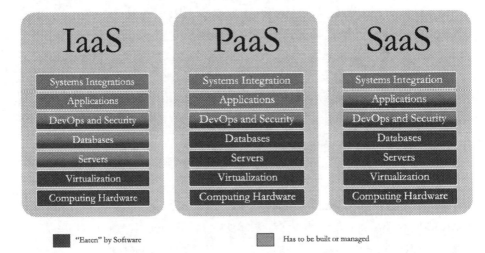

Figure 1-1. What did software eat?

The Twin Problem of Complexity and Differentiation

Besides sounding cool, what does "software eating the enterprise" even mean? It means that we have never been more capable in solving enterprise business problems with software.[10] The cloud and mobile have made it so that we can build and deploy application we couldn't have imagined 15years ago. But at the same time, we have to acknowledge that we have had no material advances that have made it easier to build software. Anyone who has been in the trenches building software intuitively knows this.

The great computer scientist Fred Brooks saw this problem even when the current software revolution was just taking off. He divided the essence of building software in his 1985 book *The Mythical Man-Month* into "essential difficulties," which come from the business or human problem you are solving, and "accidental difficulties," which are everything incidental you have to do to build software.[11]

We know from the ensuing four decades that accidental difficulties just keep increasing as the tools and technologies keep expanding. More software-based IT stack increases accidental complexity of building software. Why? Cloud software gets updated often. So you need very sophisticated development operations to stay current. The proliferation of software services, accessible over the Internet, increases the information security risk. To manage that, the specialized software that is needed now for development operations and information security has further expanded the stack. Expanding stacks make it financially impossible for most enterprises to own their entire stack. They must buy the undifferentiated part of the stack so that they can focus on building and managing differentiated parts of the stack. The decision making on buy and building in a consensus driven enterprise environments is a huge overhead. Paul Biggar concludes that this accidental complexity has become "out of control" in the cloud era.[12]

Not only has the complexity increased, the XaaS era has democratized software development. The option to buy undifferentiated building blocks is now available to everyone. That amplifies the importance of getting the layers that software can't eat right, that is, the business applications and systems integrations layers (refer to Figure 1-1). These layers are where all of the essential complexity resides—where human users interact with software.

For example, if everyone is using Twilio APIs to build a contact center, how can an enterprise company differentiate their contact center operations from their competitor using the same APIs? And if that means a contact center by itself isn't a differentiator, then the quality of the actual non-software product or service, or lack thereof, will come under spotlight. Enterprise companies now don't have to just provide a contact center. They have to imagine their product or service that feels differentiated to their customers and users. Undifferentiated business needs are already solved by the Cambrian explosion of new software vendors. The solution differentiation through creative use cases is where the new value lies.

So, the essential difficulties never go away, just as Brooks portended. You have to always spend time understanding the problem you are solving. The added need for differentiation just adds to the essential complexity of building software.

More capable software means that you have to get closer to the problem to create new value. Related to this, Benedict Evans who is an expert on the software eating the world phenomenon has a great insight. He writes that after software eats the world, "the questions that matter stop being software questions."[13] He uses retail and entertainment industries as case studies. Consider this. Hulu and Netflix have similar streaming capabilities, but Hulu isn't as valuable as Netflix. Is that more about Hulu's inferior streaming software or Netflix's superior entertainment content? Similarly, Amazon's success has made an online digital storefront a must for any retailer. But do brick-and-mortar stores don't matter anymore?

If you say yes, Target, Walmart, or Macy's may like to disagree. Maybe even Amazon may disagree, given their Whole Foods acquisition and Go store experience. The deeper point is that the questions that matter after "software ate retail" and "software ate entertainment" are retail and entertainment questions, not software questions.

The post-digital reality (i.e. after software eats the world reality) of retail and entertainment just amplifies the knotty retail and entertainment business questions. Similarly in the post-digital enterprise, the questions that matter are the ones that have always mattered for the enterprise companies. The new value resides in the business use case, creative and differentiated, not in the technology.

My personal experience bears this out. I started my career in 2003 writing software programs on an IBM AS400 system (a digitization era technology) for managing product inventory so that McCain Foods could respond to their customer demand better. Now, I and my teams build customer engagement software products for health enterprises on Salesforce and AWS (both XaaS era technologies). But on a macro level, I feel that I am solving the same problems with new (and newer) technologies. Because in the end there are only three questions important for every enterprise, big or small: how to acquire and retain customers to increase revenue, how to improve efficiency of existing operations to improve profits, and how to create a good experience for their employees and customers using enterprise systems.

Therefore, the key question to ask isn't what digital transformation to seek with the newest technology. Instead, ask what is the new way of doing business that has become possible with everything new that is available? So as Fred Brooks argued, even though *software ate the enterprise*, there are still no silver bullet answers.[11] In the post-digital enterprise, the transformation opportunity is to discover and create new business value for the same old questions, by building differentiated software solutions, and by leveraging as many building blocks as possible from what the *XaaS* ecosystem offers.

I don't think enterprises are oblivious of this imperative. Every project I am engaged with starts with an avid desire to leverage as much software *out of the box* as possible. They do a thorough evaluation of software vendors against a list of identified requirements. But the vendors are very familiar with this aspiration, and they pull out all stops to create software demonstrations that show that the boxed software can meet all the enterprise requirements to make the sale.

The issue here doesn't lie with the vendors. They are responding to the incentive. The issue lies in enterprise companies believing that what is of differentiated business value for customers is knowable in advance, as reflected in identified requirements. New business models or differentiated customer and employee experience requires more than that. It requires discovering new business use cases with working software. Instead of just "meeting" predetermined business requirements by customizing the purchased software, it requires iterating and innovating in collaboration with the customers and users. Like all great software companies do.

The enterprise companies aren't equipped to operate like a software company because they still think of software as IT, as an enabling technology. Such is the entrenched legacy of the digitization and digitalization eras. They are yet to leverage software as an innovation paradigm—the way the bleeding edge of the software world innovates in the age of software.

What Leveraging Software as an Innovation Paradigm Looks Like

Roam was on the verge of running out of money in 2017.[14] Today, it has an annual recurring revenue north of $1 million and a user base of 60,000+.[15] What happened in those four years is an incredible case study of how to innovate in the age of software.

I made notes for this book on Roam's product called Roam Research. I found out about the product initially when I saw a tweet from someone gushing about how good the tool is. Interestingly, that is how almost everyone using the tool found out about it. A Twitter user community #roamcult drove the initial adoption until it became self-sustaining. This passionate user community built websites to teach other users on how to use it. Loyal users built, and are building, plugins and workflows to automate note-taking on Roam.

I found Roam Research difficult to use in the beginning. It is a browser-based tool and doesn't have a native web or mobile app. But after I watched a few tutorials from the user community, I started loving Roam as a note-taking tool. Every note in Roam is a block that has bidirectional links to other note blocks. The problem in digital note-taking is remembering the context of each note from when you file it. Most note-taking enables tags to memorialize context. But that causes the problem of tag proliferation. Roam's links, which you can make during the writing workflow, solve that problem.

It may seem like a trivial thing if you aren't into digital note-taking. But established players like Notion are launching similar features.[16] Roam discovered and solved a need that didn't seem to exist in a crowded space of digital note-taking. Now, I don't know if Roam will succeed as a long-term business, but what they did was good enough for them to attract a $200-million seed-stage valuation.[17]

The most interesting aspect about Roam isn't the growth or valuation but their approach to innovating for their consumer use case. It leverages and relies on an open network of developers and users. Roam encourages the developer community to innovate on top of their graph database API and engages a passionate user community to drive adoption. It showcases the work of the #roamcult community and adapts ideas into the core product.[18] This model of innovation is continuous. Roam ships software updates called quality of life improvements often.[19] It is led by human capital—by the knowledge created by people using the service—while

Roam focuses on creating the graph database backbone of note-taking with bidirectional links. Even though Roam is operating at scale after initial struggle, the currency of growth isn't the economy of scale. It is the economy of scope for its niche segment of customers. There wasn't, and still isn't, a fixed plan for the product but a constant adaptation within the confines of an expansive vision—"a note-taking tool for networked thought."

Roam's story exemplifies the paradigm shift of innovation required for the age of software. This shift is there to see in the world of consumer software, and the seller side of enterprise software, but has failed to propagate to the world of enterprise software.

While what's required hasn't happened in enterprise software, the digital transformation saga just adds to the distraction. It takes the focus away from the deeper nuances of innovating with software. Without understanding software as a means to creating value, everything that gets done amounts to merely a poor imitation of what actually should get done.

Why Software Represents a Paradigm Shift

Venkatesh Rao refers to software as a "soft technology" (as quoted at the outset). He likens it to money and written language, because public cloud platforms have made software's relationship to computing hardware the same as money has to coins or credit cards or writing to paper or other media.[20]

This is no hyperbole, because there are few factors that make software a powerful general-purpose technology like money and language.

First, the cost of computing has plummeted. That makes software an attractive choice for profitable innovation for a lot more economic agents. The computing power of a modern-day iPad would have cost a typical worker in 1982 more than 360 years' worth of wages.[21]

And we can see the results of that in consumer software: when a finger tap on a smartphone can summon a car, screens recognize our faces, and late-night purchases show up at our doorstep in the morning. We also see the results on the sell side of enterprise software. We see further evidence in

13

a lot of areas where product updates are the same thing as software updates, perhaps nowhere more visible than with Tesla's over-the-air car updates. Tesla has become the biggest carmaker in part because it is better at building software than the incumbent car manufacturers. As a result, the catch-up challenge for incumbents is to make the required shift from shipping "complex cars with simple software" to "simple cars with complex software."[22] In other words, make the shift of *becoming a software company* from a car company.

This rising importance of software as an innovation medium attracts further investment. The share of software patents among overall patents filed with the US Patent and Trademark Office has grown from 5% in 1990 to nearly 40% by 2015.[23] Big software firms like Microsoft, Google, and Amazon have always been big on acquiring such patents because software is the business for them. But one should take note when a highly representative enterprise company like Capital One grows its software patent portfolio by 232% in a single year.[24]

Software is perceived, broadly now, as the substrate of the new business innovation and of improving the efficiency of existing business. It isn't just something that enables something that is another physical product. It can also be a valuable product by itself.

Finally, as exemplified by Roam, and other software-first companies, a set of clear organizational criteria and principles that are essential to leverage software for optimal business value have emerged. I described them briefly in discussion of the Roam example—open networks, continuous improvement, relying on human capital, focusing on economy of scope, dynamic customer segments, and constant adaptation.

These principles haven't emerged overnight. As per researcher and technology historian Carlota Perez, these criteria have been getting shaped since the beginning of the software revolution, which started with the invention of microprocessors in the 1970s. Perez's influential research has identified five such revolutions before software, including the industrial revolution at the end of the eighteenth century, followed by the Age of Steam Engine, Age of Steel and Electricity, Age of Oil, and Age of Mass Production.[25]

While a detailed discussion of Perez's research is out of scope for this book, it is important to highlight the three factors we have just discussed as critical to label a technology as "revolutionary"—a dramatic reduction in cost structure, increased perception of a set of technologies as ideal for innovation, and an emergence of best practice principles for business success. According to Perez, emergence of these factors indicates that a technology system has moved from "installation period" to "deployment period" of the revolution. It indicates that a technology system has become the dominant means of producing business value—what she calls "a techno-economic paradigm."

As argued here, all these factors have emerged for software. The maturation of public cloud platforms has made software into a general-purpose or a "soft" technology. The increasing software investments are evidence of its increasing perception as an innovation medium. And even though not broadly understood yet, there is a "best practice common sense" on how to leverage software for business profits. We are in the "deployment period" of software.

The Age of Mass Production required mastering mass production as a means of producing business value. The deployment age of software requires every enterprise company to master the art of leveraging software as a means of production.

Perez cautions though that unless a given company has grown up within a particular techno-economic paradigm, it is very challenging for them to execute the "socio-institutional shift" needed to succeed within that paradigm. That is the predicament for the enterprise companies pursuing digital transformation, unable to match the success of software era companies. They are unable to create outsized business value because they haven't executed their shift that Perez describes so well.

The Missing Socio-institutional Shift

To succeed in the deployment age of software, the process of value creation has to shift significantly (see Figure 1-2).

What worked for Mass Production	What works in Age of Software
Mass Production of Templates	Flexible Production and Personalization
Services became Products	Products become Services
Closed Firms	Open Networks and Platforms
Stable Routines	Continuous Improvement
Humans are Production Resources	Humans are Knowledge Capital
Rigid Tayloristic Organizations	Learning Organizations
Fixed Plans	Adaptive Guidelines with Local Flexibility
Economies of Scale	Economies of Scale, Scope, Specialization and Networks
Internationalization (Faux Globalization)	Global Economy\Local Policies (True Globalization)
Three Tier Stable Markets	Highly Segmented Dynamic Markets
No Environmental Concern	Environment is a guide to innovation

Figure 1-2. *The socio-institutional shift (Source: Carlota Perez at* `https://youtu.be/TRUlHfPLnjE`*)*

Upon a closer review of this shift, it is clear that every aspect of this paradigm shift is either facilitated with software or required due to software being the means of production.

The flexible production comes from machines that have become flexible with software-based controls. Mass personalization is made possible by extensive telemetry of customer behavior with software. And because software infrastructure for this kind of production is complex and expensive, firms have to collaborate and compete within the same networks. For instance, Salesforce and AWS are competitors, but that doesn't stop Salesforce from relying on AWS cloud for computing needs.[26] Similarly, Google pays Apple billions for running Search on Apple devices.[27]

As we have discussed earlier, modern software offers flexibility but is complex to get right. So firms have to rely on their human capital and knowledge to mitigate. The tech firms are possessive about their human talent because they realize that the value of their software comes from the knowledge capital those people hold. These firms prioritize business learning through software-based iteration. They build small multidisciplinary teams for creating innovation. Their culture places some guardrails, but the teams get the freedom to execute. It is not that these firms have more creativity, as commonly stated, but that they let their people be more creative.

We now understand that valuable software comes from adaptive iteration that solves customer and user constraints. It requires abandoning industrial planning and management (Taylorism) that enterprises still follow. Effective software management requires planning that leverages the agility of software to manage business change—with planning horizons as short as they can be. The state of the art of management sciences has moved on from Taylor's scientific principles of the mass production era, which optimized cost of production resources, to managing the framework of creative motivation of the team or teams involved.

The most creative firms tend to have missions that address the needs of real human lives and their environments. The scope of these can be big and small, but the profits are an effect of addressing real needs of individuals, institutions, and society at large.

The organizations that have executed the socio-institutional shift are reaping the benefits. The rest aren't. Perez refers to this shift as the "best practice common sense" that has to propagate across the business economy to get to the "golden age" of the software revolution.

"Best Practice Common Sense" to Become a Software Company

I am going to call Perez's paradigm shift, when applied in the context of the enterprise companies' current predicament with digital transformation, as the **software shift**.

It is the shift that consumer software and the sell side of enterprise software have already made. It is the shift that enterprise companies need to make.

I wrote earlier that enterprise efforts in this regard are a mere imitation of the principles of this software shift. To move beyond imitation, the enterprise companies need to embrace both social and institutional aspects of the shift.

It needs to happen at three different levels: technology, process, and people.

At the technology level, enterprises have to understand that transformation doesn't come from large and expensive transformation programs to implement newer and better software. Instead, it comes from new business model innovation and from building differentiated software solutions for customers and users. Vendor software offers building blocks, not to just customize, but to use it as a starting point to discover better answers to the important business questions.

Big and transformative as a metaphor for making or implementing software technology conflicts with the core essence of software development. That essence is of continuous improvement—continuously improving at the art of envisioning, building, and shipping their software.

At the process level, enterprises have to realize that bolt-on tactics like an Agile methodology and Project-to-Product don't work without the requisite cultural substrates.[28]

Just as wearing a turtleneck sweater doesn't make anyone Steve Jobs, conducting Agile ceremonies will not make an enterprise agile. The whole enterprise has to embrace the culture of agility—where teams at every level can operate at their creative best. Ultimately, Agile is about accelerating value for customers and users and requires high-bandwidth collaboration between humans creating the software and humans using the software. Waterfall methods dressed in Agile are costlier than following just Waterfall. Newer methods implemented without required cultural substrates produce organizational inertia worse than what might have existed before.

Similarly, hiring product managers or changing titles of your business analysts to product owners wouldn't result in delightful software products. The required experimentation and discovery of customer and user needs have to be a part of the cultural fabric of the business and IT teams. Business and IT stakeholders for the enterprise shouldn't be on separate teams mired in organizational politics, but part of the same small teams that are equally accountable to create the solution.

At the people level, the empowerment of small teams is foundational to hiring and retaining talent that will create great software. Enterprise still views human capital as "resources" to be optimized. But because we are scaling creation of new value with software, the "resources" framework is an anachronism. We need a "teams" framework instead. Yes, a team is made up of resources, but resources don't guarantee a team. A team forms from the shared creative motivation of people involved. A team coalesces around people who are empowered to find success. It coalesces in a culture where there is latitude to fail. A team solidifies from mutual trust.

The shift in the practices needed in enterprise is common sense everywhere else in the world of software. That is why I quite like the phrase Perez uses to describe it—"best practice common sense." There is no one magical idea but a collection of common sense–like systematic practices, which we will codify in rest of the book, that can help enterprises transcend the dogma of digital transformation and shift toward leveraging software as a paradigm of innovation. This shift is what enables an enterprise company become a software company.

The Shift Principle   Don't pursue large and wasteful digital transformations. Instead, continuously improve at building and shipping software. *Make your software shift.*

Key Tenets:

- Digital transformation is a myth. It is the trend driving enterprise IT investments over the last decade and a half, but it hasn't yielded any meaningful business transformation.

- We are in the Age of Software. Software ate the enterprise, and the source of business value in the post-digital enterprise is a good use case, not the mere adoption of new technologies.

- Each technological revolution requires mastering the means of production of that revolution. The current Age of Software requires mastering software as the means of producing value.

- For that, software should be viewed as a paradigm of innovation. That requires adopting the "best practice common sense" of creating value with software, that is, making the software shift.

- The shift can't be about big and expensive digital transformations. It has to be about continuous improvement at envisioning, building, and shipping software.

- It is a shift that consumer software and sell-side companies of enterprise software have already made and have transformed their businesses.

- To realize the promised benefits of the software revolution, enterprise companies need to stop pursuing digital transformations and make the software shift as well.

References

[1]   Rogers, B. (2016, January 7). *Why 84% Of Companies Fail At Digital Transformation*. Forbes. Retrieved March 2, 2023, from www.forbes.com/sites/brucerogers/2016/01/07/ why-84-of-companies-fail-at-digital-transformation/? sh=389e952a397b

[2]   Robinson, H. (2019, July 10). *Why do most transformations fail?* McKinsey & Company. Retrieved March 2, 2023, from www.mckinsey.com/capabilities/transformation/ our-insights/why-do-most-transformations-fail-a-conversation-with-harry-robinson#/

[3]   *The playbook for a successful business transformation*. (2020). KPMG US. Retrieved March 2, 2023, from www.kpmg.us/ insights/transforming-transformation.html

[4]   Forth, P., Reichert, T., de Laubier, R., & Chakraborty, S. (2020, October 29). *Flipping the Odds of Digital Transformation Success*. Boston Consulting Group. Retrieved March 2, 2023, from www.bcg.com/publications/2020/increasing-odds-of-success-in-digital-transformation

[5]   Vailshery, L. S. (2022, June 13). *Worldwide IT enterprise software spending 2009–2023*. Statista. Retrieved July 1, 2022, from www.statista.com/statistics/203428/total-enterprise-software-revenue-forecast/

[6]   Chu, J. (2007, March 12). *Minsky on AI's Future*. MIT Technology Review. Retrieved July 1, 2022, from www. technologyreview.com/2007/03/12/226270/minsky-on-ais-future/

[7]   Spataro, J. (2020, April 30). *2 years of digital transformation in 2 months.* Microsoft. Retrieved July 15, 2022, from `www.microsoft.com/en-us/microsoft-365/blog/2020/04/30/2-years-digital-transformation-2-months/`

[8]   Evans, B. (2020, May 29). *Marc Benioff Delivers: "The Best I've Ever Seen Salesforce Perform."* Acceleration Economy. Retrieved August 1, 2022, from `https://accelerationeconomy.com/cloud/marc-benioff-delivers-the-best-ive-ever-seen-salesforce-perform/`

[9]   Furrier, J. (2020, November 30). *Exclusive with AWS chief Andy Jassy: The wakeup call for cloud adoption.* SiliconANGLE. Retrieved August 5, 2022, from `https://siliconangle.com/2020/11/30/exclusive-aws-chief-andy-jassy-wakeup-call-cloud-adoption/`

[10] Evans, B. (February 2020). *Tech in 2020: Standing on the shoulders of giants.* Benedict Evans. Retrieved July 15, 2022, from `www.ben-evans.com/presentations`

[11] Brooks, F. P. (1995). *Mythical Man-Month, The: Essays on Software Engineering, Anniversary Edition* (20th anniversary ed., Chapter 16). Addison-Wesley.

[12] Biggar, P. (2019, February 28). *What is Dark?* Darklang. Retrieved August 1, 2022, from `https://blog.darklang.com/what-is-dark/`

[13] Evans, B. (2021, March 18). *Outgrowing software—Benedict Evans.* Benedict Evans. Retrieved August 20, 2022, from `www.ben-evans.com/benedictevans/2021/3/18/outgrowing-software`

[14] *Tweet from Conor White-Sullivan.* (2022, January 17). `https://twitter.com/Conaw`. Retrieved July 25, 2022, from `https://twitter.com/Conaw/status/1306722418786881536?s=20`

[15]   Bru, T. (2020, September 3). *The History of Roam Research and the Roamcult*. Tobias Bru—Medium. Retrieved August 25, 2022, from https://medium.com/age-of-awareness/the-history-of-roam-research-and-the-roamcult-4c1e1897633d

[16]   *Tweet from NotionHQ*. (2022, January 17). https://twitter.com/NotionHQ. Retrieved July 20, 2022, from https://twitter.com/NotionHQ/status/1306677709263630336?s=20

[17]   Clark, K., & Victor, J. (2020, September 11). *A $200 Million Seed Valuation for Roam Shows Investor Frenzy for Note-Taking Apps*. The Information. Retrieved July 30, 2022, from www.theinformation.com/articles/a-200-million-seed-valuation-for-roam-shows-investor-frenzy-for-note-taking-apps

[18]   *Roam Research Developer Hub*. (n.d.). Roam Research. Retrieved March 1, 2023, from https://roamresearch.com/#/app/developer-documentation/page/49715b-M2

[19]   *Roam Research Quality of Life Improvements*. (n.d.). Roam Research. Retrieved March 1, 2023, from https://roamresearch.com/#/app/help/page/_EqbjQSAF

[20]   Rao, V. (2018, February 8). *A New Soft Technology*. Breaking Smart. Retrieved May 15, 2022, from https://breakingsmart.com/en/season-1/a-new-soft-technology/

[21]   *Cost of Computing Power Equal to an iPad2*. (2011, August 5). The Hamilton Project. Retrieved August 20, 2022, from www.hamiltonproject.org/charts/cost_of_computing_power_equal_to_an_ipad2

[22]   Evans, B. (2018, August 29). *Is Tesla disruptive?* Benedict
        Evans. Retrieved August 20, 2022, from `www.ben-evans.com/`
        `benedictevans/2018/8/29/tesla-software-and-disruption`

[23]   Kalache, S. (2019, April 30). *The rising importance of software*
        and information technology as drivers of R&D and innovation.
        LSE Blogs. Retrieved August 22, 2022, from `https://blogs.`
        `lse.ac.uk/businessreview/2019/04/30/the-rising-`
        `importance-software-and-information-technology-as-`
        `drivers-of-rd-and-innovation/`

[24]   Panitch, G. S. (2020, December 23). *Why Everyone Is*
        Patenting Software Inventions. Finnegan. Retrieved July 25,
        2022, from `www.finnegan.com/en/insights/articles/why-`
        `everyone-is-patenting-software-inventions.html`

[25]   Perez, C. (2009, January). *Technological revolutions and*
        techno-economic paradigms. Technology Governance.
        Retrieved July 15, 2022, from `http://technologygovernance.`
        `eu/files/main/2009070708552121.pdf`

[26]   Salesforce, Inc. (2021, June 23). *AWS and Salesforce Announce*
        Expansive Partnership to Unify Developer Experiences and
        Launch New Intelligent Applications. Salesforce News and
        Insights. Retrieved July 20, 2022, from `www.salesforce.`
        `com/news/press-releases/2021/06/23/salesforce-aws-`
        `partnership-expansion/`

[27]   Albergotti, R. (2020, October 29). *Apple earnings*
        highlight search deal with Google. The Washington Post.
        Retrieved July 20, 2022, from `www.washingtonpost.com/`
        `technology/2020/10/29/apple-google-search-lawsuit/`

[28]   *Tweet from Shreyas Doshi.* (2021, May 26). `https://twitter.`
        `com/shreyas`. Retrieved May 10, 2022, from `https://`
        `twitter.com/shreyas/status/1397609770517815302?s=20`

CHAPTER 2

Create Value Through Customer Progress, Not by Meeting Requirements

The Value Principle

Software is this weird space where you can spend basically nothing and create a billion dollars of value, or spend a billion dollars and create basically no value.

—*François Chollet*

The machine itself makes no demands and holds out no promises: it is the human spirit that makes demands and keeps promises.

—*Lewis Mumford*

© Amarinder Sidhu 2023
A. Sidhu, *Becoming a Software Company*, https://doi.org/10.1007/978-1-4842-9169-6_2

> *You think you know just what your customers would like, but in reality, it can feel pretty hit or miss. Place enough bets and-with a bit of luck-something will work out. But that doesn't have to be the case, not when you truly understand what causes consumers to make the choices they do. Innovation can be far more predictable—and far more profitable—but only if you think about it differently. It's about progress, not products.*
>
> —*Clayton Christensen*

The value that can be created with software isn't a function of meeting business requirements at the lowest cost possible.

You can create billions of dollars of value with software without much cost. WhatsApp had only 55 odd employees, but it was valued at $19 billion when it was acquired by Facebook.[1] Honey Science, maker of a small browser extension that helped consumers save money, was valued at $4 billion when it was acquired by PayPal.[2]

You can also end up with little to no value at the cost of billions of dollars. GE's fall out of Dow Jones index in 2018 coincided with it spending billions of dollars on the GE Digital initiative. IBM, another behemoth of the industrial era, spent billions of dollars "transforming industries" with Watson but to no effect.

WhatsApp's messaging service had 450 million globally diverse and active users at the time of acquisition. Three hundred fifteen million of them were using it every day. Not only was the usage high; the service was adding 1 million new users a day.[3] It was a simple service allowing users to send fully encrypted multimedia messages. Honey, a small Chrome browser extension, similarly made it easy for its users to save money. While making online purchases, the service helped find discount codes or better deals at the checkout. It had 17 million active users and 100 million in revenue at the time of PayPal acquisition.

There was nothing *big* or *disruptive* about WhatsApp and Honey. But the new and differentiated value for the customers was clear and simple. Only the acquirers saw the disruptive potential, but companies themselves were just laser focused on creating value for their customer niche.

That presents a stark contrast to the journeys of two of the industrial-age behemoths, GE and IBM.

Jeff Immelt, CEO of GE, proclaimed at GE Digital's launch in 2015 that it would be a top ten software company by 2020.[4] Underpinning this proclamation was a software platform called Predix launched a bit earlier in 2013. In contrast to WhatsApp and Honey, Predix's purpose was anything but simple: "a standard and secure way to connect machines, industrial big data and people."[5] By the end of 2016, GE was on track to spend $5 billion on GE Digital.[6] When Jeff Immelt "retired" from GE in 2017,[7] GE was the worst-performing stock in Dow Jones. GE eventually split into three companies in 2021, and GE Digital was quietly folded into a combined energy and power business.[8]

IBM Watson's story is similar. After Watson's triumph in *Jeopardy!* in 2011, IBM dubbed it as "the future of knowing."[9] It was ready to position Watson's pattern matching software to a variety of fields—health care, finance, law, and academia. Unfortunately, the system designed to predict correct answers in a trivia game wasn't ready to become an all-purpose answer box in the real world.[10] Nowhere else are Watson's struggles as well-documented as in health care. MD Anderson Cancer Center partnered with IBM Watson in 2003 with a goal to automate oncology diagnosis as a part of its Moon Shots program.[11] The Watson-based software product was called Oncology Expert Advisor. After spending US $62 million on it, the project was canceled in 2016. IBM pursued many such similar software projects to develop Watson-powered health solutions. But those solutions failed to measure up to the messy reality of health care.[12] Once touted as "revolutionary," Watson Health was eventually sold off for parts in 2022.[13]

Mozilla engineer Sam Penrose is understood to have said[14] software programming is labor that creates capital. From the examples I cited, it is clear that labor that employees of WhatsApp and Honey expended created capital. On the other hand, IBM and GE's market value has shrunk by more than $100 billion each in the last decade. While all of their decline isn't due to Watson and GE Digital, respectively, they were flagship software-driven initiatives supposed to create new business value for these declining industrial-age companies. From that perspective, it would seem that GE and IBM not only failed to create capital; they ended up destroying it.

The Only Test of Value That Matters

I don't want to dunk on IBM or GE any more than what has been done already, because the predictable failure of new and differentiated value creation symbolized by their missteps within enterprise companies' software initiatives is very common, big or small.

Consider the following examples of smaller enterprise software initiatives. In 2019, Hertz filed a lawsuit against Accenture accusing them of delivering "a flawed product," exhibiting "extortionist-like behavior to fix," and breaching its contracts with Hertz.[15] This was after Hertz had hired Accenture for a $32-million digital transformation program to create an Uber-like customer experience by replacing their existing systems.[1]

The big transformation gone wrong is not only a money sink while fixing; it results in a poor experience for all the teams and developers involved. In my time within enterprise software consulting, the word quickly gets out on the street among the new hires on such projects to be avoided. These are projects where the chasm between overpromise and

---

[1] A customer can be any end user–external customer using the enterprise products or services or an internal employee using the enterprise software system to do their job. The notion of who the customer is poorly thought of in enterprise software.

under-delivery grows so wide that practitioners are scared of getting lost
in the abyss. There are numerous such examples that I can't share without
falling afoul of my current employment obligations. So let us look at
another highly public example. HealthCare.gov was budgeted to cost $93
million but ended up costing the US taxpayer to the tune of $2.1 billion.[16]
It went so far down the overpromise/under-deliver abyss that President
Obama had to lead a personal mission to recruit top engineers from Silicon
Valley to save face for the administration.[17],2

The lethal cocktail of overhyped market announcements, execution
pressures from big cost budgets, and throwing new technology on ill-
defined business problems kills enterprise software programs routinely.
While the GE Digital and IBM Watson failures were very visible, they
shouldn't be surprising to anyone who has spent time working in
enterprise software.

Therefore, we need to look at a bigger imperative. What is so different
about creating new and differentiated value in the Age of Software?
Why doesn't the tried-and-tested method of transforming existing ways
of operating with new software technologies work like it used to in the
digitization and *digitalization* eras?

Here's my explanation. For a medium as powerful as software, which
can seemingly solve all problems and is becoming more capable every day,
how well a problem is defined matters more than how a problem is solved.
Software is much closer in nature to artistic media like paint than to
engineering materials of the industrial era like steel or plastic.[14] A software
developer operates in a realm of thought like a painter. Because software
is easy to change, a lot more can be iterated in software as compared with
steel or plastic.

---

2 As reported by Jeff Lawson in his book, President Obama went into the meeting
with Silicon Valley engineers and announced, "Your country needs you."

But the history of innovation shows that just because you can build
any solution doesn't mean you should. To stay focused on creating new
and differentiated value, the development of a software solution must fit a
customer's specific and unsolved problem.

Consider the example of the steam engine technology, one with the
highest-value impact of all human inventions. The plans for making a
steam engine were available during the times of the Roman empire. But
they chose to make toys with it—opening giant bronze temple doors by
apparent magic. The steam engine as we know it, the one that heralded
Britain's industrial revolution, took shape when Thomas Newcomen
first figured out how to pump water with it out of flooded mines to save
trapped miners.[18] While Romans just bought more slave labor when
some drowned in the mines, Newcomen solved a real human problem
and ended up creating something useful for humans, that is, something
of value.

Whether it translates to something useful for humans is the only test
of the technology that should matter, however powerful the technology
may be. It mattered when Romans and Newcomen were tinkering with the
steam engines. It matters now when companies are grappling with how to
adopt latest software technologies like Generative AI within the enterprise.

Bureaucratic Visions, Mediocre Products

Creating new value requires a creative filter of customer problems that
are worth solving. Without that, as IBM and GE learned, there is a very
fine line between business visions that actually translate into something
transformative and those that merely amount to some bureaucratic
proclamation.

A bureaucratic vision often views the future as some optimal end
state and the execution as a fill in the blanks exercise with the latest and
the greatest technology. But for real transformation, you have to solve

immediate and specific customer problems that roughly conform to your stated vision. The execution itself provides the lens for identifying the most fertile directions to creating customer value. And this has to be done continuously for the actual transformative outcomes to emerge.

Related to this, let me share a conversation I had with a team prospecting technology for such a bureaucratic vision. The vision was to eliminate disease through adopting disruptive technologies. This team wanted to know if my software product could help them achieve their vision.

I was stumped by the ask initially. I had something very specific— software and APIs—to build and scale health and medical software apps. How would I even begin to bridge the gap to their vision?

But it felt like a good opportunity. I wanted to at least make an honest attempt to understand the need. So I asked them, "What does a world with no disease look like?" I got some empty stares. Then I asked if they knew of any specific gaps in the patient care that they wanted to fulfill with software. The stares continued to be empty. I tried asking the first question again, more generally this time. How did technology fit into their imagination of the new reality—or if they were focusing on a specific disease to start with?

After 15 minutes of awkward back-and-forth like that, I finally got some feedback. My software product was too narrow and context-specific. They needed something "universal." To make the vision a reality, they were looking for "exponential types of technologies." Needless to say, I never heard from that team again. It was probably for the better. I didn't have any problem with the vision actually. There is nothing wrong in thinking big. But what stuck out for me was that they never acknowledged how little they understood about making that vision real. All they were banking on was finding some technology to fill in the blanks.

Today, we live in a media culture that deifies iconic tech CEOs like Elon Musk and Jeff Bezos. If they can dream big and make incredible software products, why can't everyone else? The enterprise executives want to follow their footsteps. Aided by vendors sometimes, they come up with seductive visions like eliminating disease. Instead of identifying and understanding problems that patients face to solve, fitting such visions, they commission teams to *sense* the landscape for technologies to make their visions real.

Now, there is nothing wrong with having a big and bold vision. But a big vision without a specific and immediate road map is a recipe for mediocrity. Yes, Musk wants the human race to become an interplanetary species, but he also has the nous to build reusable rockets first. A vision must be fine-tuned by discovering what is possible with technology by executing like SpaceX is. SpaceX is testing and pushing the edge of rocket technology by delivering payloads back and forth from and to the ISS all the time. Similarly, Bezos and Amazon have revolutionized retail because they take the time to understand how to leverage technology to make the operations as efficient as possible to solve existing retail problems in unique ways.

A big and bold vision makes us feel good. Who doesn't want to eliminate disease? It has an almost moral imperative. But without investigating a specific customer (a patient in this case) problem, which aligns with that vision, and having a specific near-term road map to solve such a specific problem, that vision is merely a bureaucratic pipe dream.

Building a good road map requires you to understand what is possible in principle with the available technology. Benedict Evans provides an interesting insight on this in a blog post about predicting technology pathways.[19] He compares the Wright Flyer with the Bell Rocket Belt—the two technologies that were candidates for future commercial flights in 1962. Both looked like impractical toys at that time, but there was one crucial difference. In his words:

> *The Wright Flier could only fly 200 metres, and the
> Rocket Belt could only fly for 21 seconds. But the Flier
> was a breakthrough of principle. There was no reason
> why it couldn't get much better, very quickly, and
> Blériot flew across the English Channel just six years*

*later. There was a very clear and obvious path to make
it better. Conversely, the Rocket Belt flew for 21 seconds
because it used almost a litre of fuel per second—to fly
like this for half an hour you'd need almost two tonnes
of fuel, and you can't carry that on your back. There
was no roadmap to make it better without changing
the laws of physics. We don't just know that now—we
knew it in 1962.*

Whenever someone comes up with a big vision, they have to have a hypothesis of what they want to solve and how it aligns with what is possible with the technology. That was true when the Wright brothers were building their flying machine. It is equally true for creating software for "future of knowing" or "better customer experience." You need some hypothesis of why something big is solvable with the available technology. You need to know your breakthrough of principle.

Without it, your bold vision will invariably fail. It will not create the presumed value from implementing new technology. And despite your best intention to be transformative, your vision will only be seen as a bureaucratic objective in retrospect and yield a mediocre product.

The Distraction of Fast Galloping Horses

When software programs fail or they don't create the presumed value, enterprises start losing their confidence in building good software. The lack of execution escalates the fear of ever imminent digital disruption. Fueled further by the digital transformation industrial complex, this fear creates an effect of trying to find answers in new, and still newer, technologies. Instead of investigating, business problems are presumed. Enterprise companies look for the answer before the right questions have been fully asked.[20]

This reminds me of an old Zen story about a man riding a horse. The horse was galloping fast, and it appeared this man was going somewhere important. Another person standing along the road asked, "Where are you going?" The rider yelled back, "I don't know. Ask the horse." I believe the predicament of the rider illustrates the predicament of enterprise companies well, when they look to build value with software.

Reflecting on this metaphor, we now have fast galloping horses, coming at us every month, every week, or even daily. Microsoft popularized the concept of shipping "good enough" software initially, because they were learning by shipping. Remember those buggy Windows and Office software and the CDs we used to buy for applying yearly updates. The cloud and mobile platforms have put that concept on steroids. Software platforms are subject to constant change now. Not a day goes by without an announcement of new technology capability from the vendors. The social media fueled cheering of new technology announcements is a cultural ritual now.

It is extremely hard to not get distracted by these fast galloping horses, these tides of fast-changing options for enterprise software technology. There is a temptation to hop on one of these horses to go someplace meaningful. There is a temptation to presume technology to provide the answers on where to find new value. Evgeny Morozov calls this tendency "solutionism."[20] This tendency feeds an irrational paranoia that if enterprises keep transforming by adopting new software technologies, they can stay relevant. That way, they can avoid the ever-imminent disruption.

It creates a desperate paranoia of transformation now or bust. If you have worked in enterprise software, you may have heard this paranoia playing out to spend money on some new technology, in the immediate and the now. While I am paraphrasing, many enterprise software programs start with a shrill cry for big and urgent technology investment: *"If we don't invest big, and build this now, we will miss the market opportunity."* Enterprises go ahead and make these paranoia-driven big investments

and launch software systems. The customary congratulatory email threads
ensue. But when it comes to system adoption, all you hear is crickets. Or
the system crashes and burns many times before users can leverage it
meaningfully.

The main persuasion device within the enterprise to get technology
spending budgets is paranoia. Vendors use it. Enterprise executives use
it. It is Andy Grove's *only the paranoid survive* dictum taken to its extreme
conclusion. But if the end goal is creating software that drives real business
transformation, paranoia has to be tempered with curiosity. Curiosity
about the underlying business problem is what creates the *right* software
solutions for new and differentiated business value.

A fast galloping horse, if you don't know where you are going, just leads
you in the wrong direction faster. Similarly, applying expensive technology
to poorly defined problems, even though it may be very capable, is a huge
money sink: No technology, however capable, can create value by itself.
Good problem definition matters more.

A Short Case Against Gathering Requirements

Let us look at the state of problem definition within the enterprise next.

Within the consensus-driven enterprise environment, the
development teams don't take the time, or aren't given the luxury of time,
to understand specific customer problems. Instead, they gather customer
requirements. The problems are either presumed ("the legacy system is
inefficient," "customers need better experience," etc.), or the requirements
are categorized to abstract some understanding of the underlying problem.
Quite often, customers, or business stakeholders as they are called, aren't
even actual users or customers. They are representatives—proxies for
actual users—or are buying decision makers. In this landscape, deciding
what to build for new and differentiated value is extremely hard.

Because consensus seeking pulls in so many business stakeholders, the stakes get high. That brings high visibility and political intrigue. Executives, vendors, and development teams optimize the development project for optics. Therefore, even though the projects may start with the right intent to solve most pressing user problems, they slowly but surely devolve into a different objective: *meeting gathered requirements at the lowest cost and in the shortest time.*

There is no path to new and differentiated value with the preceding objective. I mean, *just fuhgeddaboudit.*

Let me illustrate further with a story. I was part of a program once where a large insurer wanted to create a more "customer-centric operating model." On that fuzzy vision, they attempted to execute twice and failed both times! There was no clear definition of the specific customer problems they wanted to solve. For each attempt, they started with a long list of business requirements. Both times, under cost and timeline pressures, they ended up just replicating the functionality of their old system in the new technology. The vision to create a customer-centered operation became a *migration* of their existing ways of doing things to a new technology because the optics for missing the cost and timeline estimates supposedly had career-ending consequences for some. After paying tens of millions of dollars to the vendors, they eventually decided to go back to their old system. Their learning was that their legacy system was enough to meet the business requirements in "the short term." Quite a painful and costly realization to just go back to the status quo, one might say. The executive communication noted that they now knew they "needed better tools" and that it would be "costlier and take longer than expected." The whole thing followed the big transformation gone wrong storyline to the tee.

How might this insurer have gone about their program differently? What can be an alternative to the dominant best practice of *gathering and meeting requirements at the lowest cost*? For this insurer, the critical need was to create customer solutions that provided better experience. Typical to an enterprise environment, they didn't have the specific customer problems to be fixed. What they really needed eventually with their solution was to create a better *fit* between what customers valued (better experience) and what this insurer valued (better customer services without increasing operating costs). What could they have done differently?

To come up with an answer, it is important to know what *fit* means first. Christopher Alexander, an architect and a design theorist, explores the idea in his wonderful book *Notes on the Synthesis of Form.*

In the world of design, *form* is anything humans introduce into the world, software based or otherwise. The best "forms" are the ones that have perfect fit with the "context" of a real-world problem. As per Alexander, understanding a positive (good) fit requires learning about negative instances of the fit[21]:

> *The concept of good fit, though positive in meaning,*
> *seems very largely to feed on negative instances;*
> *it is the aspects of our lives which are obsolete,*
> *incongruous, or out of tune that catch our attention.*

All possible requirements for a good customer experience, as this insurer realized, are impossible to determine, because it is always easier for us to determine what's wrong than what's right in a given situation. That is what Alexander refers to as "negative instances" of fit. He goes on proposing a process for achieving a great *fit* by iteratively eliminating these "negative instances" or "incongruities":

> *I should like to recommend that we should always*
> *expect to see the process of achieving good fit between*
> *two entities as a negative process of neutralizing the*
> *incongruities, or irritants, or forces, which cause misfit.*

Consider another non-software example, of a carpenter smoothing the surface of a piece of wood. While doing that, the carpenter often checks the wood surface with a leveler. The smoothness comes from neutralizing surface incongruities (crests) iteratively. The process for achieving smoothness is chiseling away the crests one by one. When the leveler

fits the wood surface, the carpenter has achieved their vision. Reflecting
on the carpenter's modus operandi, instead of gathering and meeting
requirements, we should focus on fixing incongruities for the customer. The
bad experiences stand out. The broken processes are impossible to ignore.

Therefore, for this insurer, the starting list of requirements shouldn't have
been all possible requirements that help achieve better customer experience.
They should have been only the ones that can result in fixing the broken
processes that result in poor customer experience, only the requirements that
can result in fixing incongruities that their customers faced.

In order to create value, the objective should never be a comprehensive
spec. It should be a *minimum spec.*[22] The managers of the developers and
teams should resist the temptation to be comprehensive. They should define
no more than absolutely necessary to start iterating on a new solution. In
addition to eliminating known and well-understood negative instances of
fit (fixing incongruities), it could include additional guardrails for regulatory
compliance or specific mistakes to avoid that involve high risk for the
business. But beyond that, the goal should be to enable the development
teams to discover and gradually evolve the product or a system that *fits* the
customer needs the best.

Focus on Progress, Not on Meeting Requirements

I hear clients frequently articulate an aspiration of providing an "Uber-
like experience" for their customers. They talk about creating "delightful
products" for their consumers. But after articulating those objectives,
instead of focusing on *incongruities* faced by their customers, they ask
developers to implement something with hundreds of requirements
gathered from customers. Instead of starting with a minimum spec, they
inadvertently pivot to a comprehensive spec.

Even if all those specs originate from customers, it can't work.
Because customers don't know what they need until they see it working.

For example, I really like closing the daily rings on my Apple Watch. Had someone in Apple's design team cared to ask me if I would like such a thing, I would have surely said no. I liked counting steps, but not much else. Before I bought my Apple Watch, I had cycled through a couple of Fitbits and a Garmin. Then maybe in an attempt to look different from the crowd, I wore an old analog watch for a little while. After that watch broke down, all I was looking for was a watch with a step counter. I had no idea about the utility of closing the rings. Similar to my revealed preference, most successful products are obvious only in retrospect, because we don't know what we want until we see it. When you inquire about a solution requirements from an enterprise customer, they will always describe it through the lens of their current way of doing things.

That is why the gathered requirements or specs can't be viewed as an agreement on what customers need. They are merely illusions of agreement.[23] The illusion is due the customer's *seeing vs. knowing* chasm. Unless the teams take the time to unpack those requirements to develop an understanding of underlying customer problems, they are just an imagination of what customers may need.

As a result, such requirements never result in a good product or solution, even when enterprise companies follow all the best practices. These days, enterprises are hiring product managers in droves to build products. They are implementing Agile software development methodologies for creating "customer-led innovation." They are implementing design methodologies like Lean UX to tide over this *seeing vs. knowing* chasm. I am afraid all these best practices, without the common sense of good problem definition, are like those fast galloping horses from the Zen story. Without focusing on fixing incongruities, these practices are merely imitative. Just as technology can't create new value by itself, best practices by themselves don't result in a valuable product.

When it comes to creating new value, it isn't even about creating products in the first place. As the great Harvard business professor Clayton Christensen has said: "It is about [creating] progress."

Christensen, in his book *Competing Against Luck,* urges developers to focus on learning "how to hear what your customers don't say." The best way to learn that is by understanding what prevents them from making progress. Christensen proposes, to innovate, builders should understand *jobs to be done.* He defines a "job" as the "progress a person is trying to make in a particular circumstance." He emphasizes understanding the customer's "circumstance." He cautioned against "functional, social and emotional" dimensions of *jobs* and *circumstances.*[24]

When creating new customer value, the source of new ideas to innovate is the constraints on customer progress. What is preventing the enterprise customer or user to do the job they are trying to make? What is constraining their progress in their day jobs? Similar to how focus on *fixing incongruities* helps define better customer requirements, *removing constraints* on customer progress helps define required solutions better. A great product is not just reusable or scalable software, as commonly discussed within enterprise environment. Great products emerge from a process of continuously creating progress in the lives of your customers by showing them working software solution.

As we have noted, technology is changing faster than ever in the Age of Software. In response, customer constraints also evolve faster than ever. Truly new and differentiated solutions come from understanding and solving for those customer constraints iteratively. That is no longer a one discrete event of gathering and *meeting requirements at the lowest cost and in the shortest time.* It has to be a constant iterative process. As we learned with the *Shift Principle,* it is a process of continuous improvement.

Once in my early career, I was tasked to build a research query software for matching patients to a clinical trial. I started interviewing researchers and data concierge teams. They told me everything about what they wanted, quite animatedly. I got some details. In fact, I was drowning in them and was getting frustrated. The principal investigator of the trial protocol sensed my struggle. He sat with me one afternoon. He walked me through clinical workflow of cancer diagnosis. He explained the process of resecting samples in a cancer surgery and their importance in cancer research. He helped arrange a live tour of their tissue bank—where the research samples were banked. I understood how a research query traced back to a banked bio-sample. I understood the process incongruities that made it hard to find patients with banked samples. I knew the constraints of the data concierge teams in accessing the right data. I wasn't fretting about definitions of data elements anymore. I had learned about the customer *jobs to be done* and discovered constraints people faced in doing their jobs.

More importantly, I discovered that my job wasn't to just gather requirements, but find new ways to make the lives of the researchers and data concierge simpler with software.

Always Be Looking to Close the Value Deficit

Creating new and differentiated business value goes beyond following the best-in-class practices or implementing the best-in-class technology. It is only realized when a customer or a user perceives the software product or services as valuable. The tricky part is that human perceptions, as we all know, are very fickle. A software solution, that a large group of humans will pay for, requires a higher ideal of human progress. It needs a minimum spec: incongruities to fix, constraints to remove, guardrails to keep, mistakes to avoid. It requires giving developers that minimum spec, and entrusting them with finding and implementing the solution for the customer's progress, and validating it by putting software in the hands of those users. And doing it continuously.

We all know that the idea of digital transformation rests on leveraging new software technologies for creating better experience and services for internal and external customers. But while building enterprise software solutions, somehow we continue to be torn between *"we know what is right for the customer"* and *"customer is always right."* We are hooked on the ideal of meeting all the business requirements at the lowest cost. We launch big transformations, instead of iteratively resolving constraints against the customer progress—the only way proven to achieve the required equilibrium for achieving a fit between what the customer wants and what the enterprise should provide in response.

This process of achieving a fit requires an extensive trial-and-error process, which at a first glance may seem wasteful in the enterprise software context, because the enterprise software management processes are tuned for optimizing cost budgets and meeting the delivery timeline. Those ideals are incompatible with value-driven pragmatic hacking needed for new and differentiated customer value. For a flexible and capable medium like software, the efficiency of execution doesn't come from optimizing costs and timelines, but from a specific focus on solving user problems as a continuous improvement exercise.

Even IBM experienced some success after they started to adhere to that principle. The Watson for Genomics product focused on a specific problem: linking a patient's genetic mutations in a file to all the relevant oncology drugs and available clinical trials. They tasted success when they embraced the goal of making the life of a researcher easier. We will never know now, but maybe with that level of specificity and long term focus across other Watson initiatives, IBM could have achieved a vision more valuable than they imagined eventually.

When a vision is fine-tuned by iteratively resolving customer constraints, it creates a value surplus similar to what WhatsApp and Honey reaped during their acquisitions. But a big vision, uninformed by actual execution and without a specific road map to solve problems, creates a value deficit right from the beginning. There was nothing deficient in the underlying technology deployed, just that the value deficit was ultimately too high within IBM's and GE's visions.[14]

When those visions invariably went unrealized, as it also did for my insurer client, a common takeaway is that they ran out of software investments. It is a fallacy and couldn't be any further from the truth. The real reason is they lost to the unmitigated complexity in the software development process that resulted from the high value deficit.

The Value Principle   Create new value through customer (internal and external) progress. Don't just gather and meet business requirements with new and newer technologies at the lowest possible cost.

Key Tenets:

- With software as a means of production, you can create billions of dollars of value without much cost. Just as easily, you can end with little to no value at the cost of billions of dollars.

- To avoid the failures in creating value, everything you build should pass a timeless test of value: new technology investments should translate into something useful for human users.

- Avoid big and bureaucratic visions for launching software programs. Instead, start by knowing your breakthrough of principle—what are newly solvable problems with available technology.

- Resist the pervasive disruption paranoia and the related technology solutionism. Instead, stay curious about the new business problems that can be solved with available technology.

- Don't start with a big list of gathered requirements through consensus. Instead, start with a minimum spec that enables the developers and teams to evolve the right customer solution.

- Ultimately, it can't be about following best practices for creating products with new technologies. It is about creating solutions that help your customers make progress.

References

[1]   Olson, P. (2014, October 6). *Facebook Closes $19 Billion WhatsApp Deal*. Forbes. Retrieved August 30, 2022, from www. forbes.com/sites/parmyolson/2014/10/06/facebook-closes-19-billion-whatsapp-deal/?sh=6c00c1845c66

[2]   Perez, S. (2019, November 20). *PayPal to acquire shopping and rewards platform Honey for $4B*. TechCrunch. Retrieved August 30, 2022, from https://techcrunch.com/2019/11/20/paypal-to-acquire-shopping-and-rewards-platform-honey-for-4-billion/

[3]   Blodget, H. (2014, February 20). *Why Facebook Bought WhatsApp*. Business Insider. Retrieved August 30, 2022, from www.businessinsider.com/why-facebook-buying-whatsapp-2014-2

[4]   *Creation of GE Digital*. (2015, September 14). General Electric. Retrieved March 7, 2023, from www.ge.com/news/press-releases/creation-ge-digital

[5]   *GE Launches 14 New Industrial Internet Predictivity Technologies to Improve Outcomes for Aviation, Oil & Gas, Transportation, Healthcare and Energy*. (2013, October 9). Business Wire. Retrieved March 7, 2023, from www.businesswire.com/news/home/20131009005749/en/GE-Launches-14-New-Industrial-Internet-Predictivity-Technologies-to-Improve-Outcomes-For-Aviation-Oil-Gas-Transportation-Healthcare-and-Energy

[6]   Mann, T., & Gryta, T. (2020, July 18). *The Dimming of GE's Bold Digital Dreams*. The Wall Street Journal. Retrieved December 23, 2021, from www.wsj.com/articles/the-dimming-of-ges-bold-digital-dreams-11595044802

[7]   Blank, S. (2017, October 30). *Why GE's Jeff Immelt Lost His Job: Disruption and Activist Investors.* Harvard Business Review. Retrieved December 25, 2021, from `https:// hbr.org/2017/10/why-ges-jeff-immelt-lost-his-job-disruption-and-activist-investors`

[8]   Loten, A. (2021, November 10). *GE Digital to Play Scaled Back Role in Split.* The Wall Street Journal. Retrieved December 25, 2021, from `www.wsj.com/articles/ge-digital-to-play-scaled-back-role-in-split-11636509584`

[9]   Kelly III, J. E. (2015). *Computing, cognition and the future of knowing—How humans and machines are forging a new age of understanding.* Public Services Alliance. Retrieved December 21, 2021, from `http://publicservicesalliance. org/wp-content/uploads/2015/10/Computing_Cognition_ WhitePaper.pdf`

[10]   Lohr, S. (2021, July 17). *What Ever Happened to IBM's Watson?* The New York Times. Retrieved December 25, 2021, from `www.nytimes.com/2021/07/16/technology/what-happened-ibm-watson.html`

[11]   *About the Cancer Moon Shots Program.* (n.d.). MD Anderson Cancer Center. Retrieved March 9, 2023, from `www. mdanderson.org/cancermoonshots/about.html`

[12]   Strickland, E. (2019, April 2). *How IBM Watson Overpromised and Underdelivered on AI Health Care.* IEEE Spectrum. Retrieved February 1, 2022, from `https://spectrum.ieee. org/how-ibm-watson-overpromised-and-underdelivered-on-ai-health-care`

[13]   Ross, C. (2022, January 21). *Once billed as a revolution in medicine, IBM's Watson Health is sold off in parts.* STAT News. Retrieved March 16, 2023, from www.statnews.com/2022/01/21/ibm-watson-health-sale-equity/

[14]   Rao, V. (2018, February 8). *Rough Consensus and Maximal Interestingness.* Breaking Smart. Retrieved May 3, 2021, from https://breakingsmart.com/en/season-1/rough-consensus-and-maximal-interestingness/

[15]   Belden, J. (2019, November 8). *5 New Significant Developments in the Hertz vs. Accenture Case.* UpperEdge. Retrieved June 20, 2021, from https://upperedge.com/accenture/5-new-significant-developments-in-the-hertz-vs-accenture-case/

[16]   *HealthCare.gov.* (n.d.). Wikipedia. Retrieved March 9, 2023, from https://en.wikipedia.org/wiki/HealthCare.gov

[17]   Lawson, J. (2021). *Ask Your Developer: How to Harness the Power of Software Developers and Win in the 21st Century* (Kindle ed., page 86). Harper Business.

[18]   Dale, H. (2022, February 23). *Meritocracy, Elite Overproduction, and A New Ruling Class.* Helen Dale | Substack. Retrieved March 9, 2023, from https://helendale.substack.com/p/meritocracy-elite-overproduction

[19]   Evans, B. (2020, May 16). *Not Even Wrong: Predicting Tech.* Benedict Evans. Retrieved May 24, 2021, from www.ben-evans.com/benedictevans/2020/5/16/not-even-wrong

[20]   Morozov, E. (2014). *To Save Everything, Click Here: The Folly of Technological Solutionism* (reprint ed., page 6). Public Affairs.

CHAPTER 2   CREATE VALUE THROUGH CUSTOMER PROGRESS, NOT BY MEETING
            REQUIREMENTS

[21]   Alexander, C. (1964). *Notes on the Synthesis of Form* (later pr.
        ed., page 19–21). Harvard University Press.

[22]   Heinemeier Hansson, D., & Fried, J. (2010). *Rework* (Kindle
        ed., loc. 633). Crown Business. www.amazon.com/Rework-
        Jason-Fried-ebook/dp/B002MUAJ2A/

[23]   Morgan, G. (2006). *Images of Organization* (new ed., pages
        114–115). SAGE Publications.

[24]   Hall, T., Dillon, K., Duncan, D. S., & Christensen, C. M. (2016).
        *Competing Against Luck: The Story of Innovation and
        Customer Choice* (first ed., Chapter 2). Harper Business.

CHAPTER 3

To Multiply Value, Mitigate System Complexity

The Complexity Principle

> *The essence of a software entity is a construct of interlocking concepts: data sets, relationships among data items, algorithms, and invocations of functions. This essence is abstract, in that the conceptual construct is the same under many different representations. It is nonetheless highly precise and richly detailed. I believe the hard part of building software to be the specification, design, and testing of this conceptual construct, not the labor of representing it and testing the fidelity of the representation. We still make syntax errors, to be sure; but they are fuzz compared to the conceptual errors in most systems. If this is true, building software will always be hard. There is inherently no silver bullet.*
>
> *—Frederick Brooks*

© Amarinder Sidhu 2023
A. Sidhu, *Becoming a Software Company*, https://doi.org/10.1007/978-1-4842-9169-6_3

Complexity, I would assert, is the biggest factor involved in anything having to do with the software field. It is explosive, far reaching, and massive in its scope.

—*Robert Glass*

Good code is code that minimizes system complexity. And system complexity is dominated by the complexity of the relationships between your system and everything it interacts with. Including people—the system users and the system developers.

—*François Chollet*

Nothing illustrates the software becoming an innovation paradigm more than the cars we drive. Tesla, the carmaker with arguably the best software, has become the most valuable car company in the world. Albeit briefly, its value, measured as market capitalization, exceeded the next ten carmakers combined in 2021.[1]

Software is driving the value of a car. It also constitutes up to 40% of the build cost.[2] Tens of millions of lines of software code see action every time you make a small grocery run. This software runs spread out over the car in components called electronic control units (ECUs). A modern car can have hundreds of such interconnected ECUs powering and controlling various features.

The proliferation of software in a car has made features like adaptive cruise control and automatic emergency braking, once considered luxury, standard. It has transformed the car from just a mode of transport into a full-fledged infotainment center. Furthermore, it enables manufacturers to keep up with safety and emission standards without increasing the cost too much. Perhaps a factor of most importance for the future, software is the primary ingredient for achieving the promised vision of autonomous driving.

It is not too much of a stretch to say that more software in the car generally means a better car. But there is a caveat. More ECUs and software increase the complexity of the *car as a system*.

Not only does each ECU have to function properly; it has to integrate well with other ECUs in the final configuration of a car. The traditional manufacturer offers many models and many variants of each model. As a result, it has to pick from and cobble together hundreds of ECUs to build a car. That results in a combinatorial explosion of the model variant configurations that have to be tested before shipping out a car.

But because manufacturers are reliant on suppliers, they have limited insight into the inner workings of each ECU. And since there could be so many final configurations of each vehicle, suppliers don't have as much insight into all the final build configurations supported by each ECU they make. As a result, interactions between these ECUs become a source of unintended systemic consequences—a key behavioral characteristic of a complex system.

A system becomes complex when its behavior can't be predicted from the behavior of its components. A lot of interconnected software-driven ECUs do that to cars. Due to this complexity, it isn't surprising that 2019 was a record-setting year for vehicle recalls due to ECU defects. And half of such recalls involved software-based defects. While software may be *eating* the car,[2] the immense complexity of shipping software with the car is *eating* the manufacturers.

One way to test the ECU configurations is to collect data from cars running on the roads. To facilitate that, cars need to be connected to the Internet. But a connected car becomes an information security risk. Paired mobile apps, cloud-based services, and electronic communications inside the car increase the "potential attack surfaces" for cyberattacks. Cars, previously designed for drivers' physical safety, now have to accommodate their digital security and privacy. Yet even more complexity.

This complexity that is rearing its head in car manufacturing is, in fact, intrinsic to software as a medium of production. Great software products and services often feel magical. But they are difficult to engineer and can even feel impossible to build if the underlying complexity isn't understood and goes unmitigated.

Complexity Ensures That There Is No Silver Bullet

Marc Andreessen wrote, or rather proclaimed, in 2011: "Software is eating the world."[3] The proclamation was prescient for the world of consumer software, at least. Today, there are very few aspects of a consumer's life untouched by the magic of software. You can almost feel it: when one tap on a smartphone can summon a car, when screens recognize our faces, when ChatGPT gives human-like answers, and when late-night purchases show up at our doorstep in the morning.

This magical quality is a reflection of the immense value, seemingly infinite, to be had when companies build great software. This magic is apparent in segments of consumer software and the sell side of enterprise software. But it keeps eluding the buy side of enterprise software—the enterprise companies. When these companies struggle to build, they believe that they don't have the resources of the big tech companies. That is only partly true. The real reason they fail to build great software is that they mismanage the complexity of software development.

What is this software complexity? Frederick Brooks defined it in two categories way back in 1975: essential and accidental.[4]

Essential complexity comes from using software to solve a real-world business problem. It stems from properties of software as a medium of construction—abstract but highly malleable.

Software is invisible, apart from what presents on-screen. This invisibility prevents us from making a mental model of its inner workings. A physical product, like a kitchen toaster, you can see and touch. You can take it apart to see its constituents. In contrast, two entirely different representations of software code can create the same on-screen behavior. This abstract nature makes it hard to visualize its working before you build it.

Software is unvisualizable. We can't have scaled-down geometrical abstractions to visualize bits and bytes interacting the way a building can be visualized as a scaled-down 3D model, for instance. We can draw diagrams for data flows or model the functions, but the reality of the way software works can't be embedded physically.

Inasmuch as we can't see or visualize it, we have to describe software to be built by the concept of a function it will perform. That is why the hardest part in software development is defining what to build. Customers can only know what they want when they see it working. Even though they may indicate an agreement on functional concepts, it is impossible for them to fully confirm their needs by looking at functional specifications. Due to this inherent abstractness, it is impossible to avoid "conceptual errors" in software that gets built. As a result, a software system has to be updated and revised many times to fit customer needs.

Discovering and iteratively solving these conceptual errors constitutes the irreducible essential complexity of software. Brooks referred to it as the ***essence*** of software.

Accidental complexity comes from the process of producing software.

On top of the essence, you have to make a dizzying amount of additional choices for the actual build of production-ready software. Paul Biggar, the founder of CircleCI, a software integration and deployment platform, describes the challenge as follows[5]:

> *Fundamentally, writing software is just receiving*
> *data, manipulating it, storing it, and sending it*
> *somewhere—easy concepts that we learn in our*
> *first programming tutorials. Why is it that to build*
> *an application today we need to learn Kubernetes,*
> *Docker, Git, load balancers, dozens of AWS services,*
> *SQL, NoSQL, Kafka, Unix, GraphQL, gRPC, npm,*
> *Heroku, DNS, memcached, JWT, Nginx, and the rest*
> *of the endless list of tools and technologies that each*
> *provide one part of an application?*

The choice of technologies and tools is not the only type of accidental complexity. Developers and teams have to stay abreast of hundreds of best practices, which are constantly evolving. And when building large-scale software systems, there is the complexity of human interactions between developers and between different development teams. Brooks described the work required to manage, reduce, and eliminate this accidental complexity as the ***accident*** of software.

While we have become more capable with software, the essence hasn't gotten, and will never get, easier. The accident, even after all the software innovation, and as Biggar explains, has simply "gotten out of control." I mean, there are multibillion-dollar companies just to solve some aspect of the overall software accident, for example, Atlassian, Gitlab, and even all the XaaS platforms.

So, if the consumer software examples I mentioned at the beginning seem magical, it is only because those software companies eliminate the accident as much as possible so that they can enable their human talent to focus on building for the essence. What may seem magic is someone else's painstaking and diligent engineering.[1]

---

[1] Robert Heinlein said about this: "One man's 'magic' is another man's engineering."

Writing back in 1975 at the dawn of the Age of Software, Brooks concluded that he saw "no silver bullet" when it came to increasing productivity in software development. His remarkable assertion has stood the test of time really well, even when you consider the recent AI advances for producing basic code. While consumer software companies and enterprise software vendors may understand this, at least the successful ones, enterprise companies, coming to terms with building their own software systems, don't.

Building Systems Is Like Navigating Tar Pits

La Brea in California has ancient, natural, and preserved tar pits. Natural asphalt has been oozing into these pits since the end of the ice age. It is understood, from the fossil records, that prey animals and pursuing predators wandered, got trapped, and died in these tar pits.

In *The Mythical Man-Month*, the book that also outlines the "no silver bullet" insight, Fred Brooks likened building large software systems to the struggle of animals that might have been trapped in La Brea tar pits in prehistoric times[6],[2]:

> *Large-system programming has over the past decade*
> *been such a tar pit, and many great and powerful*
> *beasts have thrashed violently in it. Most have*
> *emerged with running systems—few have met goals,*
> *schedules, and budgets. Large and small, massive*
> *or wiry, team after team has become entangled in*
> *the tar. No one thing seems to cause the difficulty—*
> *any particular paw can be pulled away. But the*
> *accumulation of simultaneous and interacting*
> *factors brings slower and slower motion. Everyone*
> *seems to have been surprised by the stickiness of the*
> *problem, and it is hard to discern the nature of it.*

---

[2] I find the imagery of trapped animals so evocative of the struggles of enterprise companies that I was compelled to visit these tar pits.

Just like his amazing foresight on the irreducible software complexity, the preceding observation from Brooks holds true for enterprise software many decades later. Building enterprise software systems continues to feel like navigating tar pits. Large and small teams stretch constantly to meet schedules and budgets, and very few of them meet their goals.

Enterprise software is mainly building bespoke systems leveraging the available vendor technologies (refer to Figure 3-1). A software system, even when composed of many technologies and products, has its essence and accident. The accident is making all the component technologies and products work together as a single and unified production system. The essence is using the final system to solve specific business problems. The tar pits manifest because the enterprise companies ignore the essence and accident of building good systems.

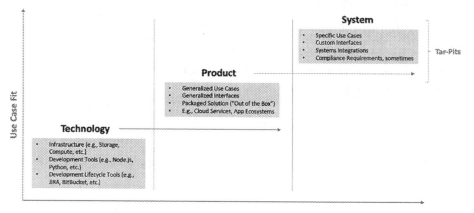

Figure 3-1. *Systems, complexity, and tar pits*

Startups, venture capitalists, and vendors providing off-the-shelf software allege that enterprise companies are slow at software-based innovation. Enterprises assert, in their defense, that startup and vendor software doesn't measure up to their unique use cases. Both sides are right to some extent, but gloss over a critical nuance.

In reality, software vendors overstate the fit of their products for bespoke enterprise systems that are eventually needed while selling and marketing to the enterprise. Despite the market narratives claiming as such, we know that the XaaS era hasn't really solved the key problem of the enterprise companies needing to build their own custom software for their specific use cases.

On the other hand, enterprises get overzealous in acquiring *fully* turnkey solutions. They underestimate the complexity of leveraging new technology to solve their specific business problems and build a working production system.

Therefore, both sides underestimate the accident and oversimplify the essence.

As we looked at in Chapter 2, IBM's lack of success with Watson Health was because they couldn't create a system powered with Watson that could fit into real-world medical practice. They got entangled in the tar:never got to building the essence, and just remained stuck in the accident. In the same vein, the struggle of traditional carmakers with software-based recalls is a struggle in the tarpit as well, as is the struggle of enterprise companies with large digital transformation programs.

The Holy Trinity Problem

There is an often-repeated software truism about scope, timeline, and quality: you can only pick two of the three. If you insist on getting software with a fixed scope delivered on a predetermined timeline, it is quite likely it will be of poor quality. So on and so forth. I call this the Holy Trinity Problem of software development.

I have never been on a project where a team solved this problem, unequivocally. Yet, I see enterprise executives and software managers glossing over and exhorting teams to solve it. And when software projects invariably fail, they discuss how cost, timeline, or scope was mismanaged. They fail to see how cost overruns, project delays, or unintended consequences on scope are all effects of mismanaged software complexity. It's because a large majority of them, specifically the ones who have never written software code themselves, only know how to manage scope, timeline, or quality. They don't understand the relationship of these variables with complexity of the software system.

Even developers know about this complexity only in their lived experience. They lack the vocabulary to explain it to people higher than them in the corporate hierarchy. As a result, there is a communicative divide between the two camps. Executives and managers believe that developers always misrepresent development estimates. Developers always pad their estimates because they know that the scope outlined in the early and uncertain phases of a project is always unrealistic. Both sides never communicate around reducing the accident so as to focus on solving the essence.

At this juncture of discussion, I should quickly note that something complex is different from something complicated. A complicated problem is hard, but is solvable with a recipe. It can be solved with deploying a known process or an organizational structure, like an industrial-style command-and-control structure. *Digitization* and *digitalization* era IT projects were complicated, but they were never complex. Even if you got one or more of the variables of the holy trinity wrong, which happened often, you can solve the resultant challenges by expanding budgets and throwing more people at the project or riding the development teams hard to get things done because what needs to be done is fairly well understood.

Where things are now within the Age of Software, following a recipe doesn't guarantee new and differentiated business value in outcomes. The unique value lies in leveraging available software to discover and build to solve novel use cases for customer progress. That is a complex problem. There is no recipe to follow.

Both IBM and GE (our Chapter 2 case studies), for their respective Watson and GE Digital initiatives, spent a lot of time and money. These industrial era beasts thrashed in the tar pits with all their might. But the essence and accident of deploying software systems against the real-world problems, such that it creates new business value, got the better of them. There were too many unknowns and too many interrelated factors, which prevented them from executing those initiatives with an industrial-style command-and-control approach. In other words, they mismanaged the complexity of building the software system.

To solve the seemingly mystical problem posed by the holy trinity (the symptoms of the problem), it is critical to find and flex the tactical levers that can mitigate the complexity (the core problem).

The antidote to complexity is simplicity. To *become a software company*, enterprise companies have to find and flex the levers for simplicity in their software development lifecycle (SDLC), the levers that can reduce the accident to create focus on solving the essence.

To identify and understand the simplicity levers (the complexity antidotes), let us go back to our example of Tesla to see how they do it. They are a car company that started as a software company. What lessons can we draw from how Tesla operates for enterprise companies trying to become software companies?

Stop Wasting Time on "Build vs. Buy"

When people refer to modern cars as computers on wheels, they are only partially right, because in reality, these cars are a mishmash of many computers since ECUs are supplied by many different suppliers. These computers are black boxes, are hard to integrate, and proliferate the wiring harnesses required. To avoid this problem, Tesla engineered a simpler software system—a single software platform that controls all functions.[7] This platform system architecture is what enables integrated controls on a single tablet-like screen within a Tesla.

The other manufacturers are scampering to copy this single-screen interface. Almost every car now boasts a large flashy touchscreen. But these manufacturers are functionally constrained by the complexity of the hodgepodge of many ECUs. Therefore, the traditional manufacturers can catch up with Tesla, but only if they simplify their software system architecture. Also, Tesla manages the model variant combinatorial explosion by offering fewer models of hardware and structuring the in-model variations through software.

Tesla built a system to minimize the *accident* of building good software for cars instead. Tesla created the *most simple system* (MSS) first that provides them differentiation against the incumbent car manufacturers. In comparison, traditional manufacturers are just trying to meet requirements with the lowest cost possible, buying the ECUs they need to build the car from the low-cost suppliers.

What can we learn from this?

Similar to the traditional car manufacturers, consider the "build vs. buy" decisions that enterprise companies make for their system buying decisions. These decisions have outlived their utility. An analysis needed for the Age of Software is what software should an enterprise rent, buy, reuse, or build to create the MSS. A system that can enable them to iterate and try variations quickly. This analysis is not one or two big discrete decisions. It is a large number of micro-decisions to build a software development that can provide a foundation for agility.

A salient outcome of the software revolution is the explosion of software marketplaces and application ecosystems for enterprise business software. But as we discussed in Chapter 1, while more options are available, the accident of building software systems has increased by expanding software stacks. Therefore, it makes sense to tap into marketplaces and ecosystems to buy and reuse software that others have built.

But each such decision doesn't need a big "buy vs. build." Instead of procuring systems, identifying the right suppliers you can consistently work with for pieces of your stack is a more relevant analysis. That requires a lot of smaller decisions to acquire software components with the objective of enabling the MSS—to reduce the accident and enable a higher agility for innovating on higher-value use cases.

Optimize Your Software Stack for Agility

While traditional manufacturers are still only innovating with software at the level of infotainment systems, Tesla can rapidly test and launch features around battery efficiency, auto-piloting, and self-driving due to its MSS. Tesla's software stack allows them to control everything, from batteries and motors to the AC and the navigation, with software.[8] It is clear that Tesla has invested in creating a stack to leverage software's actual agility, while there is little evidence that other manufacturers have cracked the code for that.

Software code is easy to change—that is the foundational source of agility. But as we see from the Tesla example, that agility has to be unlocked by building the right software stack. Without such a dynamic and flexible stack, it can take weeks—sometimes even months—to implement small system changes, as I have often seen with enterprise clients.

When the system lacks modularity, a change in one component causes a ripple effect elsewhere in the system. ECU dependencies, and resultant software defect recalls, in a car are a prime example. When ignored, beyond the defects, the lack of modularity can even make the interactions between various teams building large systems complex and slow the development down, thus reducing the agility.

Amazon ran into this challenge when it was expanding fast in its early days. Jeff Bezos instituted the "Two-Pizza Rule" to create smaller teams.[9] Each team had to be of a size that it could be fed by two pizzas. Each team managed a part of the system with an interface that other teams could interoperate with. Now commonly referred to as API-based services architecture, it is an example of an architecture pattern to reduce the accident of software.

In my domain of work, clients often aspire to create an "Uber-like" delightful experience for their consumers. While they can easily see Uber's clean and simple user experience, they don't see the foundational strength of system architecture Uber has invested in. Uber has more than 2,000 application microservices that power the few screens that consumers see.

What is perhaps more important is what they are trying to enable with this architecture. They are making their system "more flexible" to allow developer teams to be "more autonomous."[10] The interfaces of each service or of each domain of services create specific constraints on how the system can be built and extended. But each team managing the service or domain of services can be more creative with what they can do.

So, one aspect of reducing the accident within your software stack is the good architecture. The second is the quality of your development infrastructure. Software companies, like Google or Facebook, typically spend up to half of their development budgets on state-of-the-art infrastructure to write code, test, and deploy software changes in the production system rapidly.[11] It is something that customers will not ask for directly in requirements you gather, but to create something customers would find delightful has to be part of your stack.

Good infrastructure is a nonfunctional requirement that becomes functional when you are trying to innovate quickly for your customers. Think Tesla's over-the-air updates and the delight they create for drivers. That ain't possible with a great software delivery infrastructure.

Within enterprise software, it is unfortunate that the notion of design has narrowed down to just visual design or some high-level veneer to connect a hodgepodge of disparate applications. But good system design that unlocks the true agility inherent in software requires optimizing your entire system stack. Modular architecture and good infrastructure are critical to reduce the accident of building software and result in responsive software systems—ingredients often found missing in the broken and static stacks of the non-software companies.

Think Big, Iterate Small

For Tesla, as the technology and their understanding of the solution's fit improve, shipping improved vehicle performance is synonymous with shipping a software update. They ship a lot overtime, but each update is small and iterative.

There is a related insight we can draw. My clients, sometimes, argue that it is difficult to be iterative when the software is regulated. Even for that, Tesla is showing how. The transportation industry is as regulated as it comes, and differently across jurisdictions. Tesla doesn't plan for regulation as just a compliance requirement to meet. They see it as a constraint to be solved with software iteratively.

Take the example of the Autosteer feature. Yes, it is a far cry from full self-driving (FSD), but by offering it to drivers with safeguards—like making it unavailable when drivers don't check in at the steering wheel regularly—they are making progress toward the FSD goal. Even if they never get to it, they will get to something that is much better than the current state, while the other manufacturers don't even have a path because they lack the stack to iterate in small batches.

Tesla's approach illustrates Richard Hamming's "no fixed problem nor a final solution" mindset.[12] The mindset frees the teams from the arbitrariness of "meeting requirements on a fixed timeline." As long as they keep solving for user constraints in small increments, they can rest assured that their solutions will be considered delightful. In Chapter 1, we defined it more technically as the software shift that enterprises need to make—prioritizing "continuous improvement" over "stable routines," adhering to "adaptive guidelines with local flexibility" instead of "fixed plans," and shifting to "flexible production" with software rather than industrial era "mass production." This mindset shift toward iterating in small batches is the biggest opportunity of improvement for reducing complexity for enterprise companies.

While it is difficult to implement for enterprises, it is not a novel idea. In 1975, Fred Brooks had the following to say about the impossibility of building a satisfactory system from a specification written in advance[13]:

> *Much of present-day software acquisition procedures rests upon the assumption that one can specify a satisfactory system in advance, get bids for its construction, have it built, and install it. I think this assumption is fundamentally wrong, and that many software acquisition problems spring from that fallacy. Hence they cannot be fixed without fundamental revision, one that provides for iterative development and specification of prototypes and products.*

Yet, here we are in 2023, and enterprises are mired in the same process traps. Yes, they might follow Agile methodologies, allegedly so. They have more people employed with "product" in their titles and designations than ever. But they haven't been able to crack the nut on iterating in small batches.

Iteration is not just splitting a big project of premeditated scope into many weekly sprints. Instead, it is a mechanism for experimentation, and learning from experiments, needed for any creative exercise. Just like a scientist validates a hypothesis by gathering evidence, software iterations must be in service of validating a solution hypothesis. No Agile sprinting amounts to anything worthwhile, if this experimental aspect is ignored.

That is because the raw material for software is ideas. Modern software is so capable that the number of possible ideas is large. The only way to find out which ones will work is by testing them with the customers. To solve for the essence requires a solution that fits a customer's needs. For that, one needs to evolve the ideas that work and discard the ones that don't work, in small batches.

Allow Your People to Create

Tesla's simple systems' architecture, great software infrastructure, and iterative solution approach reduce the accident of software and help navigate tar pits of complexity that make traditional manufacturers struggle. What's even more amazing is how it relies on talented people to solve for the essence of the first mass-market software-driven electric vehicle.

When we think about Tesla, Elon Musk is likely the first name that comes to mind for most people. It's true that Elon is a one of a kind innovator. But behind Elon, Tesla's products draw on the creative work of many pioneers. Take Ian Wright, for example, who created the software architecture that is fundamental to Tesla's ability to innovate at the pace of a software company.[7] Another story that doesn't get talked about often is how Elon teamed with Martin Eberhard and Marc Tarpenning to license AC Propulsion's electric drivetrain technology before launching Tesla.[14] Or another one of how the distinctive Tesla interior looks, where everything feels in sync with its software-first approach, is a creation of Franz von Holzhausen.

While explaining about how to solve for the essential complexity of software (the essence), Fred Brooks framed it as[15]

> *The central question of how to improve software art centers, as it always, on people.*

I like how he used the qualifier art for great software design. That means the software solutions your teams build transition from good to great when developers and teams express their internal creativity, like it happened with contributions of Wright, Eberhard, Tarpenning, and von Holzhausen at Tesla.

The reason that some software firms are such magnets for human talent is that, besides being good paymasters, they provide a cultural substrate and implement management structures that allow their people to be their most creative. Within such cultures, software management isn't about estimating "units of build work" and "staffing resources" to deliver on a project plan.

The complex essence of software makes it such that no amount of such planning is foolproof. All software specifications, or software user stories as we like to call them now, are an abstraction. No matter how good you write (and good writers are not common in the software world!), it is impossible to describe what you have imagined in your head by words.

Therefore, a specification or a user story is merely an illusion of agreement. Because of that, there is no other bigger source of complexity in software development than the definition of what to build. As a result, for everything it decides to build, an enterprise has to rely on their human talent to remove the illusions of agreement by making things real.[16]

Ultimately, great talent working at their creative best develops great software solutions, not some resources who were handed a spec to deliver. A development team doing creative work takes time to build in-depth understanding of the customer's needs. From that understanding stems the belief that they can create the right solution for the need. When empowered to create right solutions, they perceive the opportunity to create software as something that will help them grow. That creates the shared anticipation of the better future they are creating with their product.

Need, belief, opportunity, and *anticipation* are creative attractors that create the perception of "meaningful work."[17] And meaningful work is the real source of creative motivation. People like von Holzhausen, Wright, Eberhard, and Tarpenning will never work for you if you just assign them assembly-line work. They love to solve for the essence.

Therefore, managing software as creative work means asking teams to solve problems, instead of asking them to "meet requirements within a fixed timeline." It means empowering your teams to build the right solutions, rather than viewing them as resources to be staffed or allocated. For developing great solutions, as Brooks is suggesting, software development has to elevate to a form of art—creative work over industrial era command-and-control assembly-line work.

Mitigating Complexity Multiplies Value

The levers of simple software development—the most simple system, a stack optimized for agility, iteration, and allowing creative work—are derived from the ideas that Brooks explained many decades ago. I adapted them for the additional context of enterprise software and for the nuances of the current times. These ideas have stood the test of time because they are fundamental to engineering great software-based systems, which all enterprises are trying to build with their software investments.

Richard Hamming, a mathematician and a computer scientist, provides my favorite definition of systems engineering[12]:

> The heart of system engineering is the acceptance that
> there is neither a fixed problem nor a final solution,
> rather evolution is the natural state of affairs.

It captures the predicament of enterprise companies trying to become software companies rather well. They have to shift from software IT, where the objective is to implement software to run business, to software systems engineering, where the objective is to iteratively solve customer problems.

That would require them to recognize and manage the software development complexity. It requires them to minimize or eliminate the accident of software so that the enterprise company's human talent can solve for the essence of software.

They have to abandon the purist approach to managing software programs and adopt a more pragmatic alternative.[18]

When scope is large and the development resources scarce, the purist approach—characterized by extensive planning and elaborate documentation—crops up. It may feel comforting when viewed against risk of execution but becomes a source of negative surprises from the complexity gods symbolized by the holy trinity, that is, cost overruns, timeline delays, and poor quality.

A pragmatic alternative, the evolutionary approach internalized and leveraged by successful software companies, is concerned with making steady progress without worrying about optimal end scope. The approach focuses on minimizing the accident by starting with MSS and optimizing the stack for agility. On top of this, the developers can focus on solving for the essence by solving customer problems iteratively, working in small batches.

The Complexity Principle   Software can generate seemingly limitless value, but it is complex to get it right. Always look to minimize the system complexity to multiply value from your software investments.

Key Tenets:

- Software as a medium of production has an inherent complexity. It is exemplified in the struggle of traditional car companies trying to become software companies.

- Software system development has two types of complexity: accidental and essential.

- Accidental complexity comes from the process of producing software—from the dizzying amount of choices to be made for tools, processes, and technologies. It is called the accident of software.

- Essential complexity comes from the abstraction required in representing a real-world business problem to solve with software. It is called the essence of software.

- Despite all the software innovation, the essence never got or will never get any easier. And the accident has simply gotten out of control. As a result, there is no silver bullet. To create great software, you need great systems engineering.

- The challenges of enterprise software systems engineering lie in underestimating the accident and oversimplifying the essence, both on the parts of enterprises and software vendors.

- Enterprise software management primarily focuses on eliminating cost overruns, project delays, or unintended consequences on scope. But they fail to understand that all of them are symptoms of mismanaged system development complexity.

- Instead, enterprise software management should focus on reducing the accident so that companies' people can help them solve for the essence of developing software systems.

Reducing the Accident

- They must stop wasting time on outdated analyses like "build vs. buy." Instead, they should build the most simple system (MSS) that can help reduce the accident.

- They must build a software development stack that is optimized for agility. This stack should have right architecture and required infrastructure to leverage the software agility.

Solving for the Essence

- They must always build in small batches and adopt the "no fixed problem nor a final solution" systems engineering mindset. Iterations should prioritize experimenting and learning about how to solve customer problems.

- The software solutions enterprise teams build transition from good to great when developers and teams are allowed to express their internal creativity. The enterprise software management should create a culture that allows people to be at their creative best.

References

[1]   Richter, W. (2021, October 26). *Tesla's Market Cap (Gigantic) v. Next 10 Automakers v. Tesla's Global Market Share (Minuscule)*. Wolf Street. Retrieved March 17, 2023, from `https://wolfstreet.com/2021/10/26/teslas-market-cap-gigantic-v-next-10-automakers-v-teslas-global-market-share-minuscule/`

[2]   Charette, R. N. (2021, June 7). *How Software Is Eating the Car*. IEEE Spectrum. Retrieved June 1, 2022, from `https://spectrum.ieee.org/software-eating-car`

[3]   Andreessen, M. (2011, August 20). *Why Software Is Eating the World*. Andreessen Horowitz. Retrieved July 26, 2020, from `https://a16z.com/2011/08/20/why-software-is-eating-the-world/`

[4]   Brooks, F. P. (1995). *The Mythical Man-Month: Essays on Software Engineering, Anniversary Edition* (20th anniversary ed., Chapter 16). Addison-Wesley.

[5]   Biggar, P. (2019, February 28). *What is Dark?* Darklang. Retrieved March 17, 2020, from `https://medium.com/darklang/the-design-of-dark-59f5d38e52d2`

[6]   Brooks, F. P. (1995). *The Mythical Man-Month: Essays on Software Engineering, Anniversary Edition* (20th anniversary ed., page 4). Addison-Wesley.

[7]   Morris, C. (2017, November 30). *How Tesla brought a systems approach to the automobile*. Teslarati. Retrieved July 13, 2022, from `www.teslarati.com/tesla-automobile-systems-approach-charles-morris-book/`

[8]   Morris, C. (2021, July 9). *What Makes Tesla So Unique And Popular?* InsideEVs. Retrieved July 9, 2022, from `https://insideevs.com/features/519228/tesla-unique-features-popularity/`

[9]   Lawson, J. (2021). *Ask Your Developer: How to Harness the Power of Software Developers and Win in the 21st Century* (Kindle ed., page 35). Harper Business.

[10] Gluck, A. (2020, July 23). *Introducing Domain-Oriented Microservice Architecture*. Uber Engineering Blog. Retrieved March 31, 2021, from `www.uber.com/blog/microservice-architecture`

[11]   Lawson, J. (2021). *Ask Your Developer: How to Harness the Power of Software Developers and Win in the 21st Century* (Kindle ed., page 247). Harper Business.

[12]   Hamming, R. (2020). *The Art of Doing Science and Engineering: Learning to Learn* (hardcover ed., page 370). Stripe Press.

[13]   Brooks, F. P. (1995). *The Mythical Man-Month: Essays on Software Engineering, Anniversary Edition* (20th anniversary ed., page 200). Addison-Wesley.

[14]   Urban, T. (2015, June 2). *How Tesla Will Change The World—Wait But Why*. Wait But Why. Retrieved July 9, 2022, from https://waitbutwhy.com/2015/06/how-tesla-will-change-your-life.html#part2

[15]   Brooks, F. P. (1995). *The Mythical Man-Month: Essays on Software Engineering, Anniversary Edition* (20th anniversary ed., page 202). Addison-Wesley.

[16]   Fried, J., & Heinemeier Hansson, D. (2010). *Rework* (Kindle ed., loc. 633). Crown Business. www.amazon.com/Rework-Jason-Fried-ebook/dp/B002MUAJ2A/

[17]   *Why CEOs are failing software engineers and other creative teams*. (2020, June 17). iiSM.org. Retrieved September 16, 2020, from https://iism.org/article/why-are-ceos-failing-software-engineers-56

[18]   Rao, V. (2018, February 8). *Purists versus Pragmatists*. Breaking Smart. Retrieved May 3, 2021, from https://breakingsmart.com/en/season-1/purists-versus-pragmatists/

PART 2

Creating Business Agility from Software Agility

As an enterprise, optimize your technology foundation, organizational culture, and development processes to leverage software development agility to create business agility as described in the following principles.

CHAPTER 4

Don't Procure Software; Create a Dynamic Stack Instead

The Stack Principle

The quality of the digital supply chain is going to determine the winners and losers in the ongoing technological era. In order to adapt, enterprises should look to build high quality digital supply chains that allow them to rapidly iterate.

—*Jeff Lawson*

To the economic question "Why is software so expensive?" the equally economic answer could be "Because it is tried with cheap labour." Why is it tried that way? Because its intrinsic difficulties are widely and grossly underestimated.

—*Edsger W. Dijkstra*

© Amarinder Sidhu 2023
A. Sidhu, *Becoming a Software Company*, https://doi.org/10.1007/978-1-4842-9169-6_4

Software engineering is about building automated systems, and one of the first things that gets automated away is routine software engineering work. The point is to understand what the right systems to reuse are, how to customise them to fit your unique requirements, and fixing novel problems discovered along the way.

—*Li Hongyi*

On April 19, 2021, a small robotic helicopter completed the first powered flight on a planet besides Earth. The helicopter's name was Ingenuity, and it was operating as part of NASA's Mars 2020 mission.[1]

The same day, GitHub placed the Mars 2020 Helicopter Mission badge on the profiles of 12,000 developers who contributed to open source software projects and libraries used by Ingenuity[1] (see Figure 4-1).

None of the software developers themselves knew that they had contributed to the software that NASA's Jet Propulsion Laboratory (JPL) had used to build the flight control software for Ingenuity. It was GitHub that took the initiative and worked with JPL to identify all the developers who contributed. They wanted to "make the invisible visible."

Figure 4-1. *Mars 2020 Helicopter Mission Badge placed on GitHub developer profiles*

---

[1] You can watch the video of Ingenuity on YouTube: www.youtube.com/ watch?v=wMnOo2zcjXA

The "invisible" refers to a fact, not well-known outside the developer communities, that modern software is powered primarily by open source software. GitHub, a leading code repository provider for collaborative development, estimates that 99% of the software systems shipped today rely on open source components.[2] Even more significant, the biggest backers of open source projects are the big tech companies.[3] The software innovation at the cloud and Internet scale has flattened the playing field so much that even big tech has to rely on open source innovation. Whether it is for NASA building flight control software for Mars with F Prime or for Google enhancing its commercial AI services with TensorFlow, open source projects are driving the leading edge of software innovation.

Now, I must note that open source software is no panacea. Quality-wise, it isn't shrink-wrapped "in-a-box" software that most enterprise buyers prefer. Despite the plentiful open source innovation, there is often a need for commercial software for buyers who don't have the wherewithal or have the need to make raw open source software legible for their purposes.

But even the state of the art of commercial software—cloud-based services accessible through web-based APIs—exemplifies how reusable building blocks drive an agile innovation in modern software.

Enterprises need to store, query, and access consumer data, but few have the need to manage the cloud infrastructure like AWS. Even Salesforce, a successful software company, uses AWS for its cloud infrastructure.[4] Many companies have to send and receive payments over the Internet, but a very few can establish compliant networks with banks at a scale that Stripe has, so much so that even the mighty Amazon uses Stripe's services.[5] Not many can specialize in building integrations with telecom companies like Twilio to ensure a phone call works anywhere a customer goes. Therefore, it was a no-brainer for Lyft to rely on Twilio to build its provider- and driver-facing experiences.[6]

Salesforce-AWS, Amazon-Stripe, and Lyft-Twilio are examples of how software platforms driving differentiated customer experience need dynamic software stacks sourced from an open network. A dynamic stack involves building on open networks and platforms, a requirement for making the software shift for enterprises. Suppliers like AWS, Stripe, and Twilio have created valuable business around the undifferentiated heavy lifting,[7] so that Salesforce, Amazon, and Lyft can focus on creating new and differentiated customer experiences, so that they can focus on their respective economies of scope, scale, and specialization, another requirement for the software shift.

Recognizing and Avoiding the Ritualistic Tribal Bloodletting

Presenting a stark contrast to these agile and dynamic stacks of Salesforce, Amazon, and Twilio, the state of the-art for enterprise software procurement processes can feel as woefully anachronistic.

Enterprise software procurement processes are known to be brutal, anything but nimble and dynamic. Martin Casado, a partner at VC firm Andreessen Horowitz, calls the sales cycle with an enterprise company a "baroque tribal ritual bloodletting."[8]

I have gone through the enterprise sales cycle many times. And I couldn't agree more.

It is baroque because enterprise software and services procurement, much like the baroque seventeenth-century European and New World art and sculpture, is extravagantly ornate. It starts with an RFI.[2] An RFI is a procurement step to collect information from potential vendors of software or software services. Even though an RFI is a preliminary step, it can still have hundreds of questions across domains like vendor information, prior

---

[2] RFI stands for Request for Information.

experience, solution details, financials, etc. This RFI process can take months to complete, and the only purpose is to down-select vendors and collate a set of premeditated business requirements from the submitted responses.

These requirements become the start of the next layer of process: the much dreaded RFP.[3] Similar to the RFI process, the RFP process could take a few more months to execute and contains elaborate questionnaires with hundreds of technical and functional requirements. An RFP is followed by presentation sessions with vendors called orals. Orals are meetings that can have 50–60 people listening and filling their assessment on how complete a vendor solution is for each listed requirement.

I have been in countless such orals. The theater around these meetings can be downright absurd at times.

The formal RFIs, RFPs, and presentation meetings are just the visible part of the iceberg. The worst of human tribal behavior happens hidden behind the scenes. It manifests as the process gets closer to final decisions. Since the core business problem is never described at a level of specificity needed to make a clear decision, the final decision boils down to who trusts whom among the various tribes that form across vendors and buyers. There is a palpable sense of *"us vs. them"* between business and IT stakeholders.[9] Occasionally, the dissatisfaction with the IT performance is so high, shadow IT teams spring up and throw their hats into the fray.[4] These teams aided by their business sponsors fight fiercely for their relevance and survival in the vendor selection process.

The vendors learn to exploit the uncertainty and mistrust. On the official RFI and RFP responses, the modus operandi is to respond with the barest minimum so as not to miss the cut for the next round. They

---

[3] RFP stands for Request for Proposal.

[4] To circumvent perceived or actual limitations of solutions provided by centralized IT, business lines build their own IT teams, called shadow IT teams, to suit their specific or urgent requirements.

combat vagueness of requirements with equal and opposite misdirection. Their sales specialists learn to demo software that doesn't exist into an art. Vaporware and "smoke and mirrors" demos, while everyone rails against them, are still very common. While this is happening, the sales executives engage in extensive backroom maneuvering and deal making outside the official evaluation. The amount of mental blocking and tackling around key decision makers, and the cringeworthy psychoanalysis that goes along, can be soul numbing if you care about real problem-solving and actually building good software.

Often, I have seen the quantitative results of the process being swept aside and the selection made in the end purely based on contacts and relationships. All said and done, the thoroughness of RFIs and RFPs is merely faux rigor and organizational drama to keep the procurement departments happy. To borrow a phrase from the king of drama Shakespeare, it is a tale full of sound and fury signifying nothing.[10]

That is why Casado isn't wrong to call enterprise software procurement ritualistic bloodletting. It is completely orthogonal to the purpose of creating a dynamic software stack we talked about in the beginning. And what's more troublesome is that by the time software is procured, and the enterprise system goes into production, it is already obsolete.

My argument isn't for enterprise companies to suspend all rigor they have codified in selecting software or software services partners. The current process may still be applicable in certain problem domains of enterprise software where the recipe for creating value is well understood, even though those domains are shrinking in the Age of Software.

By pointing out the futility of the traditional software processes, I want to emphasize that when it comes to building software for rapid customer-facing innovation, a dynamic software stack like the ones JPL and API-first companies exemplify is the only one that works.

The Urgent Need for Better "Sense-Making"

For the reasons that were probably relevant 20 years ago, the enterprise procurement processes were designed for optimizing cost. Enterprise software was IT that was leveraged for *digitizing* or *digitalizing* the business workflows. The use cases for accruing value were predictable.

Moving from paper-based to digitized records, the elements of value were well understood. For digitized workflows, doing metrics-oriented operations management is also a predictable value creation exercise. Therefore, a management framework that sought to optimize cost for the software procured worked because a model of predictability in business outcomes existed.

In the Age of Software, when the new value comes from differentiated employee or customer experience or from innovative business models, there is no such predictability in business outcomes. The experimentation required for discovery, validation, and realization for specific business outcomes makes the new value creation a complex exercise.

As we discussed within the Value Principle, just optimizing cost (meeting requirements at the lowest cost possible) for a software solution to a complex problem never really ends up optimizing cost in actuality. Worse, it may even end up destroying value as we learned from GE Digital and IBM Watson examples.

The persistent deviations like cost overruns, timeline delays, and unintended consequences are a result from a poor fit of the cost optimization model to the uncertainty that exists in the emergent business outcomes in the Age of Software. As a result, enterprise executives and managers need to apply better "sense-making" when selecting software and software services vendors.

Let's look at a related framework called Cynefin (pronounced kuh-NEV-in). It is a business "sense-making" device developed by Dave Snowden and is an effective framework to right-size software procurement methods vis-a-vis problems to be solved (Figure 4-2). Cynefin means habitat in Welsh. So the name literally means "understand your habitat." It offers five different domains of decision-making context.

Obvious represents the domain of "known knowns." The cause and effect of a problem is clearly understood such that a best practice can be applied to solve the problem. For example, I don't need a plan to drop my kid at school every morning. The drop-off time is fixed, and the route is the same every day. Most days, my reflexes guide me.

Complicated represents the domain of "known unknowns." The decision-making context is such that the system can be broken into constituent parts and system behavior can be predicted by modeling the constituents. Teaching computers to play chess falls in this domain.

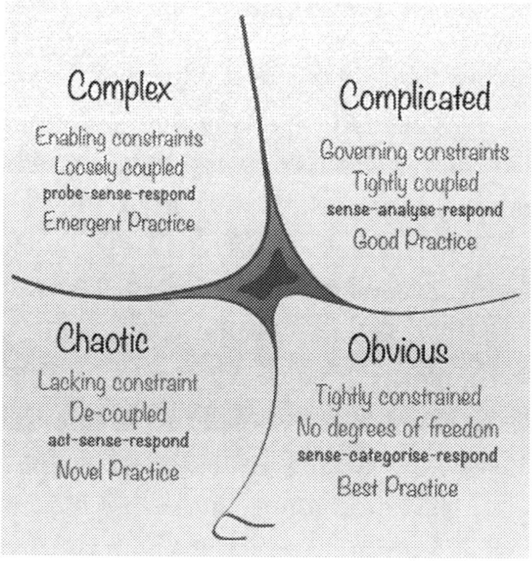

Figure 4-2. *Domains of the Cynefin framework, the dark domain in the center is confusion (Source: Dave Snowden, released under CC BY 3.0)*

Complex represents the domain of "unknown unknowns." This decision-making context requires probing through experiments to discover unknowns. The interactions between constituents of a system cause emergent behavior such that system behavior can't be predicted by modeling the constituents. When reductionist models that assume predictability are applied to a complex system, the results can be drastic, for example, market crashes that happened due to lack of circuit breakers in trading algorithms in 2008.

Chaotic domains simply have no cause and effect relationship. You can't even wait to learn from system feedback. It is important to just act and then adjust based on results and by studying new information. Government lockdowns in response to rapidly spreading COVID-19 are an example of an action in an environment of chaos.

Disorder is a state of confusion in the middle, where any other domain doesn't apply. By definition, it is difficult to identify. The only way out could be to break into many parts and apply domains as appropriate. The disorder of broken mask and ventilator global supply chains needed multiple different responses—airlifting supplies from China (chaotic domain), building local supplies (complicated domain), and people building their own masks (obvious/clear domain).

The Problem Domains of Enterprise Software: What Makes Sense?

These domains can also be used for "sense-making" in the context of building a dynamic software stack.[11]

A new consumer app for health behavior modification will fall into the complex domain. To achieve a fit to user needs, it needs quick cycles to understand what consumers value through feedback on working software. A system error corrupting the entire database falls in the chaotic domain. It requires quick action to stop bleeding before you do anything else. A playbook-based routine, like routine software upgrades, doesn't require any methodology. It falls in the obvious domain. Building an integration across two ERP systems is complicated for an experienced team, but may get complex for a team that doesn't understand those systems.

A given management situation may move across domains. In the consumer app example, validating the app with customers for achieving the market fit is a complex domain problem. However, once you have the core problem identified and a fitting solution discovered, launching and scaling an app is a complicated domain problem.

While optimizing costs can work for a complicated problem, doing that for a complex problem only has two very predictable outcomes.[12] Like HealthCare.gov, software technology programs can either become runaway train wrecks—it was initially estimated to cost $93.7 million by the supplier, but ballooned to $2.1 billion in a rather publicized way—or become programs that end up in a state of gridlock, like some of my clients that complain about their IT teams or their vendors: *"They can't seem to get anything done."*

When faced with a complex business problem, a dynamic software stack (based on open networks and platforms, exemplified by JPL and API-first companies) acts like the necessary buffer against runaway train wrecks or gridlocks. And it allows the enterprise company to innovate at exactly the pace needed for a given program.

How to Think About a Dynamic Software Stack

We discussed the Complexity Principle and that the antidote to complexity is simplicity. We will leverage that idea again to think through how to create a dynamic software stack.

To deal with complexity in software, the Agile Manifesto authors gave a beautiful definition of simplicity in software[13]:

Simplicity—the art of maximizing the amount of work not done—is essential.

This definition is one of the 12 principles of the Agile Manifesto. I find it intriguing that they chose to call creating simple software an art, not a science. In doing so, they hinted at the futility of becoming agile by just following best practice methods or scientific analyses. I will get to the methods in detail later in the book. For now, let's just focus on the analyses—more specifically the *build vs. buy* to make supply-side decisions for procuring off-the-shelf software and software services.

Buy now means both "buying" and "renting" software.[5] More and more routine software engineering is getting automated every day. As a result, more software is becoming available to just rent, eliminating the need to buy for on-premise use. Name any major line of business (e.g., HR, ERP, finance), there is a *SaaS* company to provide cloud-based software to run the business. *PaaS* platforms allow companies to build their own cloud-based applications, for example, Twilio for contact center and Stripe for banking. If you would rather not depend on *SaaS* or *PaaS* companies and want to own more of the stack, then public cloud platforms like AWS, GCP, and Azure enable you to build your own cloud application. Beyond that, you can even set up your own server racks by buying hardware from Dell or HP.

Build now means both "reusing" and "building" software. Before building, developers have to reuse as much as possible from the open source ecosystems. And while building, software features built should be only the ones that fix a specific end user problem. It should be something that eliminates *an incongruity*, something that results in clear *progress in the job* a user or customer is trying to get done. The scope can't be a big list of requirements, but more like a minimum spec we discussed in the Value Principle.

Therefore, the art that Agile authors are referring to lies in deciding what *not to build* as opposed to what to build, by *minimizing the amount of work not done*, because you know, to really innovate for your use cases,

---

[5] *Buy* software is something with one-time cost for an on-premise use. *Rent* software is something that you access as a cloud-based service.

you must build. But it is hard to know everything you will need to build in advance. The trick is therefore to only build what you absolutely have to, following from the minimum spec idea.

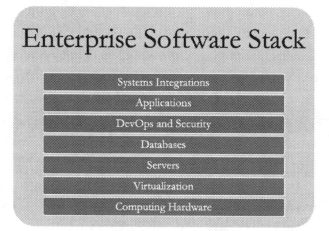

Figure 4-3. *Points of differentiation*

But to know your minimum spec, you need to understand your customer demand deeply, not just analyze the supply of technology solutions that the traditional procurement mindset emphasizes. Consequently, instead of a few big and irreversible supply-side analyses like *build vs. buy,* enterprise companies have to continuously improve at making a large amount of smaller and easily reversible demand-driven micro-decisions. Also, there shouldn't be a requirement for one stack for all enterprise systems, as sometimes IT departments start mandating. You should rationalize as much as possible. But ultimately each system should have a stack that maximizes the agility of that system and minimizes that work not done for that system.

I call these rent, buy, reuse, and build (RBRB) decisions. A dynamic software stack is an emergent outcome of making good RBRB decisions. The dynamism of your stack is a function of how small and reversible your specific RBRB decisions are. In short, it is an outcome of good sense-making to start and agility of decision making to get it right overtime.

Creating and Continuously Improving Your Software Stack

RBRB decisions can't be looked at as once-and-done types of decisions anymore. They must be continuously monitored as the business circumstances change and revised as needed. For example, when building a new customer or employee experience-related system, the bottom two layers of the software stack (see Figure 4-3) are almost always undifferentiated for most enterprise companies, except for maybe governments or as required by some regulatory requirement around data privacy and residency. Similarly, the top two layers are almost always where much of the experience differentiation happens because, as we discussed in the Shift Principle, these are layers software finds difficult to *eat*.

As a result, when starting out, any part of the stack that is not material to the differentiated user value should be the candidate to buy or rent. But some parts of the stack that may not be differentiating at a smaller scale could become differentiating at a larger scale. For example, the cloud subscription costs (rent costs) often increase with volume of usage. And at full scale, subscription costs may even become prohibitive. I have seen examples of my clients paying a single vendor like Salesforce tens of millions of dollars.

So, even if it may be a good idea to rent a part of the stack up front, there may be a need for a different RBRB decision in the future, that is, build the part of the stack on your own. Hence, there is a need to keep the RBRB decisions small and easily reversible.

A great, and related, example from the consumer realm is online streaming services like Netflix. They build their own content delivery networks now on top of public cloud providers like AWS so that a viewer in Budapest can enjoy super-popular shows like *House of Cards* with the same latency as a viewer in Los Gatos.[14] The dynamic content delivery network wasn't a differentiating need for Netflix in the beginning. But it has become now, so they decided to build their own.

All this discussion is to underline how the good 'ol *build vs. buy* analysis, still popular within enterprise companies, is way past its use by date and how it needs to be replaced with a different focus on the dynamism of the overall stack. Traditional procurement is an example of an industrial-age process that has become a mistake in the Age of Software. It is a mistake embodied in the enterprise software procurement jobs. And it is really hard to fix because highly motivated individuals in the procurement departments want it to continue.

But we know enterprise software problem domains have changed toward being more complex. The software doesn't need to be just procured anymore. It needs to work in a stack that has to be dynamic. And the stack has to respond to change quickly as business and customer needs evolve. The type of micro-decision making, and the volume of it, can't be supported by centralized procurement.

Therefore, enterprise companies have no choice but to decentralize the RBRB decision making. The guiding framework for these decisions must serve only one purpose for agility: *"maximize the amount of work not done."* The reason to "maximize the amount of work not done" isn't to avoid work, but to always stay focused on the work that creates the most customer value.

Get Technical *And* Ask Your Developers

RBRB decisions needed to build a dynamic software stack can't be cost minimizing. They have to be value-creating decisions. But to make good RBRB decisions, at a scale and frequency required for an enterprise company, they have to follow a prescription from the Shift Principle: "adaptive guidelines with local flexibility."

Maximizing the amount of work not done is an adaptive management guideline. Within that, allowing the developer teams to make their own RBRB decisions is the local flexibility.

It starts with better sense-making for problem domains and required solutions. Since value with modern software comes from embracing the possibilities rather than crunching numbers, the executives and managers have to understand the technical possibilities better. They must stop being averse to getting technical or getting into details.

Among the enterprise software management, I hear people often use the term "technologist" to describe themselves. I also observe a lot of aversion to being labeled as "technical." Both words—*technologist* and *technical*—have their origin in the Greek word *technê*. *Technê* means an art or a skill. A technical person is skilled in the craft of making something—in our case, a person skilled at making software. Technology combines *technê* with a word-forming element *-logy*. *-logy* means discourse about a subject. A technologist is someone who can engage in a discourse about *technê*.

Therefore, to become a good technologist, you must become technical first. The best technologists I have known are always the ones who have had significant technical experience in their careers. More often than not, even though they may not do technical day jobs anymore, they maintain a deep curiosity and dabble in techniques of making things with software. It is not necessary that all technical people become great technologists. But all great technologists have to be good technically.

The world of enterprise software is replete with managers and executives who call themselves technologists but aren't technical. Not only that, they don't want to get technical. Technical work to them is details— the blue-collar work of software. They don't view it as *a source of capital*, as Sam Penrose advocated that we should. The *art-of-the-possible* discourse from such technologists is often unmoored from what is technically possible. They merely borrow from and are swayed by the discourses and marketing literature of the software vendors.

To clarify, I am not arguing that enterprise managers and executives should learn software programming. I am saying that they should build their own, and within their immediate teams, the required technical expertise for effective sense-making of what's possible with what's available. While they can manage a complicated domain problem (implementing ERP software) just by managing resources and budgets, they will not be able to do it for a complex domain problem, for example, health and medical software or digital product companions.

Executives and managers can create good adaptive guidelines only by understanding the details, by being technical and good technologists. On top of that, they must provide the flexibility to their teams to make the local decisions.

I like Jeff Lawson's suggestion for local flexibility—ask your developer[15]:

> *As you build your software development team, the fundamental ask of your developers, your architects, and your technical leadership is to pick the right areas to build.*

Deciding which parts of your stack are differentiating to your customers now extends to building blocks that are not just functional but also technical. They extend deep into the always expanding enterprise software stack. When the imperative is to accelerate customer-focused innovation, wherever required, executives and managers must *get technical* themselves and *ask their developers* to make and revise the micro-RBRB decisions.

A Dynamic Stack Avoids Rituals and Prioritizes Value

Having been in the enterprise software world for my entire career, I do believe most enterprise companies care about building good stacks for software innovation. It is only when they are exposed to the scope of the decision-making—the sheer amount of it—that they revert to the default of cost optimization.

To deal with the predicament, they have to trust the respective simplicity lever we discussed in the Complexity Principle: iterating in small batches. It will seem excruciatingly slow to start, but once you get your dynamic stack built and functioning, the positive effects will start compounding.

Providing a differentiated customer and employee experience is a complex domain problem. The right solution requires iterative development, where each iteration is an attempt to understand the problem and develop a solution in small increments. Therefore, you need a software stack that enables the enterprise company to build the most simple system (MSS) to start iterating.

Getting technical yourself and asking developers to make RBRB micro-decisions is the first step. To align with the preceding imperative, what are the other process changes in an enterprise company?

To answer, we have to acknowledge an existential constraint. It isn't always possible for the enterprise companies to bring every aspect of the software development team in-house, as often advocated. Relying on vendors and service providers is a reality some can't avoid. Therefore, they also have to determine how to retain the systemic knowledge while sourcing parts of the stack, because the real software product and solution is the knowledge within the software system.

First, when defining the requirements for vendor selection, there should be clear delineation between the routine and differentiated needs for development. At the very minimum, the enterprise company needs to have the staff that can make that determination of differentiated needs, instead of asking the vendors in RFIs. The starting assumption must be *reuse* or *build* for differentiated needs and *buy* or *rent* for routine or undifferentiated needs.

As much as possible, the in-house teams should analyze the business requirements to understand the core problems. They should create a minimum spec before involving vendors, because without understanding the core problem and the traceability to business value, there can't be any prioritization required for effective iteration—everything will just seem urgent.

Second, rather than asking software vendors to respond to every requirement, ask them how they will solve for the minimum spec. And ask them how they will help the enterprise company minimize the amount of work not done. Every successful vendor has looked at the part or whole of the same problem that the buyer is trying to solve. They have made the determination to productize for some needs vs. the others, at least the successful ones. Their willingness to share that learning, on what their product doesn't solve and why, will be a good indicator on their reliability as a partner.

For the software service providers, instead of asking them the estimated cost of implementing and customizing software, only ask them to describe how they will achieve the MSS in the shortest time possible to start iterating. Because asking vendors to provide a foolproof estimate during the most uncertain phase (i.e., RFI or RFP) is akin to kicking the can down on dealing with complexity. The best answers have to be the ones that minimize development complexity. They should resonate with the themes we outlined in the Complexity Principle: starting simple, building an agile stack, developing in increments that enhance learning, and managing creative work. The winning answer should also include how the knowledge of the final system will be institutionalized within the enterprise company, the client.

Instead of running a procurement process, which feels like bloodletting, the enterprise companies have to select dynamic stack partners that provide the shortest path to building the most simple system, that is, select supplier partners, not procure software from vendors. They have to select software stack services partners that show the path to value with MSS and reduce the complexity of the software program. To make it all work, the ownership of the stack has to reside in-house in a team empowered to make the RBRB decisions.

Agility Doesn't Come in a Vacuum

There is no trend that has captured the imagination of the enterprise software world more than Agile software engineering. That is understandably so, because software as a medium of construction is flexible and very changeable. And the core premise is that changeability should yield higher velocity in solution development and accruing business value.

In real practice, however, there is a lot that has to happen between a line of software getting written or changed and a working solution that creates business value. A customer has to see progress in their day job or their life when they use the solution. As we learned with the Value Principle, creating progress requires knowing what prevents customers from making progress. This discovery and definition of the elements of user progress has to be the default underpinning of the business requirements.

But it doesn't mean creating more elaborate specifications for building, as enterprise software development defaults to. The user-facing innovation for differentiated customer and employee experience requires a certain amount of trial-and-error process—an iterative discovery and validation of customer needs through working software. That makes it paramount to get to the MSS and let the real value emerge through iterating on working solutions.

In the sense that it enables rapid user-facing innovation, a dynamic software stack, even though requiring a lot of technical and functional RBRB micro-decisions, is the foundation of true business agility. It makes an enterprise company rise above the limitations of rote methods that wrongly conflate agility with fast delivery. It makes it adaptive to the constantly changing needs of customers. More importantly, a dynamic software stack enables an enterprise to internalize the underlying agility of software by unlocking the power of iteration.

The Stack Principle   Don't procure software through one-off buy or build analyses. Create a dynamic and differentiated software stack that minimizes the amount of internal development work. A dynamic stack is the foundation of agility.

Key Tenets:

- Open networks exemplified by open source ecosystems and API-first companies drive the cutting edge of innovation in the Age of Software. They demonstrate how dynamic software stacks are a foundation of true agility.

- In contrast, the traditional enterprise software procurement processes are anything but dynamic. Some have even called it ritualistic and tribal bloodletting. These processes are completely orthogonal to the purpose of creating a dynamic software stack.

- Enterprise executives and managers need to apply better sense-making to align software buying decisions with the problem domains.

- Enterprise software programs for new and differentiated value fall in the complex domain.

- When faced with a complex business problem, a dynamic software stack acts like the necessary buffer against programs becoming trainwrecks or gridlocks.

- To build a dynamic software stack, enterprise companies have to continuously improve at making a large amount of smaller and easily reversible demand-driven micro-decisions, instead of a few big and irreversible supply-side analyses like *build vs. buy.*

- These decisions are rent, buy, reuse, and build (RBRB) decisions. A dynamic software stack is an emergent outcome of making your RBRB decisions. The dynamism of your stack is a function of how small and reversible those decisions are.

- The amount and frequency of RBRB decisions requires decentralized decision making. It requires executives and managers to provide adaptive guidelines but vesting the flexibility to make decisions with developers and teams.

References

[1]   Friedman, N. (2021, April 19). Open source goes to Mars. The GitHub Blog. Retrieved June 3, 2021, from https://github.blog/2021-04-19-open-source-goes-to-mars/

[2]   Finley, K. (2021, April 14). *Open Source on Mars: Community Powers NASA's Ingenuity Helicopter.* GitHub. Retrieved June 3, 2021, from https://github.com/readme/featured/nasa-ingenuity-helicopter

[3]   Swanner, N. (2019, August 5). *Big Tech Controls Many Major Open Source Projects. Is That a Problem?* Dice. Retrieved March 20, 2023, from www.dice.com/career-advice/open-source-google-microsoft-apple-github

[4]   Salesforce, Inc. (2021, June 23). *AWS and Salesforce Announce Expansive Partnership to Unify Developer Experiences and Launch New Intelligent Applications*. Salesforce. Retrieved March 20, 2023, from `www.salesforce.com/news/press-releases/2021/06/23/salesforce-aws-partnership-expansion/`

[5]   Nickelsburg, M. (2017, August 1). *Amazon quietly starts using Stripe to process some e-commerce transactions*. GeekWire. Retrieved March 20, 2023, from `www.geekwire.com/2017/amazon-quietly-starts-using-stripe-process-e-commerce-transactions/`

[6]   Twilio Inc. (n.d.). *How Lyft uses Twilio Flex to build trust and deliver exceptional rider and driver experiences*. Twilio Customer Stories. Retrieved March 20, 2023, from `https://customers.twilio.com/249/lyft/`

[7]   Singer, J. (2021, January 26). *Twilio and the Magic of Undifferentiated Heavy Lifting*. The Flywheel Substack. Retrieved March 29, 2021, from `https://theflywheel.substack.com/p/twilio`

[8]   Weinberger, M. (2016, June 18). *Selling software to big companies is a "baroque tribal ritual"* … Yahoo. Retrieved March 20, 2019, from `www.yahoo.com/news/selling-software-big-companies-baroque-143000391.html`

[9]   Craig, G. (2016, May 16). *Us vs. Them: The IT/Business Divide*. Planview Blog. Retrieved March 20, 2023, from `https://blog.planview.com/us-vs-them-the-it-business-divide/`

[10]   Shakespeare, W. (n.d.). *Tomorrow, and tomorrow, and tomorrow*. Poetry Foundation. Retrieved March 20, 2023, from `www.poetryfoundation.org/poems/56964/speech-tomorrow-and-tomorrow-and-tomorrow`

[11]   Ogilvie, M., Smart, J., Rohrer, S., & Berend, Z. (2022). *Sooner Safer Happier: Antipatterns and Patterns for Business Agility* (Kindle ed., page 47). IT Revolution Press.

[12]   Rao, V. (2018, February 8). *Agility and Illegibility*. Breaking Smart. Retrieved May 3, 2021, from https://breakingsmart.com/en/season-1/agility-and-illegibility/

[13]   Agile Alliance. (2001). *Principles behind the Agile Manifesto*. Manifesto for Agile Software Development. https://agilemanifesto.org/principles.html

[14]   Nair, M. (2017, October 17). *How Netflix works: the (hugely simplified) complex stuff that happens every time you hit Play*. Medium. https://medium.com/refraction-tech-everything/how-netflix-works-the-hugely-simplified-complex-stuff-that-happens-every-time-you-hit-play-3a40c9be254b

[15]   Lawson, J. (2021). *Ask Your Developer: How to Harness the Power of Software Developers and Win in the 21st Century* (Kindle ed., page 45). Harper Business.

CHAPTER 5

Implement a Strategy of Business Agility, Before the Agile Methods

The Culture Principle

> *The Agile movement is not anti-methodology, in fact, many of us want to restore credibility to the word methodology. We want to restore a balance. We embrace modeling, but not in order to file some diagram in a dusty corporate repository. We embrace documentation, but not hundreds of pages of never-maintained and rarely-used tomes. We plan, but recognize the limits of planning in a turbulent environment.*
>
> —*Jim Highsmith for Agile Alliance*

Success has many fathers, and agile innovation has a colorful heritage. While agile's complex family tree sometimes provokes passionate debates among agile practitioners, two

A. Sidhu, *Becoming a Software Company*, https://doi.org/10.1007/978-1-4842-9169-6_5

*things are clear: first, agile's roots extend far beyond informa-
tion technology and, second, agile's branches will continue to
spread to improve innovation processes in nearly every function of every industry.*

—*Darrell Rigby, Jeff Sutherland, and Hirotaka Takeuchi*

*If some of your tasks do not contribute to the desired result,
they are not worth doing. Specs, schedules, plans, or presenta-
tions are not usually the result. Likewise, meetings, reviews,
and administration are not the result. While these things can
contribute to achieving the result, they often devolve into self-
sustaining adjunct activities that contribute less than they cost.*

—*Michele and Jim McCarthy*

In 2001, a group of 17 self-proclaimed organizational anarchists met at
Snowbird in Utah and changed the world of software. They authored the
Agile Manifesto.

Before the meeting, the attendees were uncertain if they would be
able to achieve anything substantial. But they did achieve something and
ended up surprising themselves. Jon Kern, one of those authors, summed
up their achievement pithily in 2017: "Four measly bullets, and all this shit
happened."[1]

With "bullets," Kern was referring to the four core Agile software
development values[2]:

1. *Individuals and interactions over processes and tools*

2. *Working software over comprehensive documentation*

3. *Customer collaboration over contract negotiation*

4. *Responding to change over following a plan*

And a little bit regarding "all this shit" that happened, today, there is hardly any company of a meaningful size that doesn't have some Agile transformation underway. Not unrelated to that, Agile coach has become one of the fast-growing job categories. With or without Agile coaches, if you are a software developer, you must have been part of some form of Agile rollout by now. But even if you haven't been, it is unlikely that you haven't heard about it. Because even when companies don't use any specific Agile methodology, the underlying ideas like continuous improvement, small-batch development, and customer-focused development expressed in Agile Manifesto are foundational to modern software development. A narrative excerpt from an *Atlantic* feature summarizes the adoption of Agile as follows[1]:

> *Representatives from Spotify and eBay confirmed*
> *that both companies currently use Agile, and there's*
> *a job listing on Twitter's website for an "Agile Coach."*
> *Bread-crumb trails across the internet suggest that*
> *many other big-name technology companies have*
> *at least experimented with it in the past. And it's*
> *not just Silicon Valley: Walmart reportedly began*
> *experimenting with Agile years ago. The Agile*
> *Alliance, a nonprofit that promotes the use of Agile,*
> *counts all sorts of corporate giants—including*
> *Lockheed Martin, ExxonMobil, and Verizon—among*
> *its corporate members.*

But despite this widespread use, there is a cloud of discontent. The world of Agile software development is split across two polarized camps—management and developers. Managers love Agile. They are thrilled to mandate Agile processes to increase the pace of software development. Developers, depending upon the amount of process they are subjected to, either hate it or are just indifferent to it. They put up with the processes to please the management, but otherwise life goes on. It's not surprising that these two camps happen to be at the opposite ends of the totem pole of an organizational power structure. Because of that, within the enterprise environment, Agile doesn't even come close to resolving the problem that its authors thought it would[3]—the imposition of "irrational demands through the imposition of corporate power structures" that prevent "delivering good products to customers."

The Agile authors who were happy with what they drafted back in 2001 are much less sanguine today about how Agile values and principles have been adopted. Kent Beck thinks Agile is a "devastated wasteland."[4] After leaving Facebook over "irreconcilable differences," Beck was working on a course on "how technologists can use influence constructively in relationships with power differentials." Martin Fowler believes much of Agile in practice is faux-Agile[5]— "agile that's just the name, but none of the practices and values in place." Martin is annoyed that "the project management people" have taken over Agile, leaving "the technical people and the technical ideas" behind. Jon Kern has "kinda stepped out of the Agile ring"—exhausted that so many people didn't get it. van Bennekum laments the so-called Agile coaches "absolutely not knowing what they are talking about."[1]

We must note that all the 17 Agile authors were *technical people*. Therefore, their angst against the nontechnical people for poor adoption of their cherished values, or the management leveraging Agile to enforce the very power structures they were against, is understandable.

But it will be foolish to dismiss these concerns just as gripes of technical people against nontechnical people, that is, the management, or, to view the differences on Agile between management and developers as yet another illustration of an eternal struggle within corporate power hierarchies. It is a huge imperative to get Agile right within the enterprise because the philosophy of Agile, so neatly encapsulated in the four values and 12 principles of the Manifesto, is critical to unlock software as a paradigm for innovation.

Alistair Cockburn, one of the Manifesto authors, notes that it is merely "an accident of history" that it was the programmers who "decoded" something this profound about "pure mental, team-based activities" with Agile. He is right because Agile has a broad value beyond software. And the business world has woken up to the importance of Agile beyond software development.

Actually it may not even be an accident of history as Cockburn calls it. The business world isn't waking up now. It had been implementing the fundamental ideas behind the Agile movement to make groups effective since much before the programmers decoded it.

A Random Walk Down Agile Street

The Agile Manifesto drafted in 2001 was a culmination of a sequence of events that started before World War II. With increasing access to computing, the software world had already started experimenting in making development more Agile. For example, when the Internet Engineering Task Force (IETF)—an international community that maintains the standards behind the evolution of the Internet—formed in 1986, they chose their motto as "rough consensus and running code." The same philosophy was later encapsulated as a core Agile value: "working software over comprehensive documentation." Furthermore, *Agile* was merely an adopted name for values and principles embodied in several "light" or "lightweight" software development methodologies that existed before 2001.[3] The word itself was borrowed from the title of a book,[6] *Agile Competitors and Virtual Organizations*. The book reviewed examples of companies that were creating new ways of adapting to changing markets in the 1990s.[7]

One of those lightweight methodologies, Scrum, a clear winner of the methodology wars after the Agile movement took off, was invented in 1995 by Jeff Sutherland and Ken Schwaber (two of the 17 original Agile authors). Scrum didn't originate in isolation. It was modeled on a capstone concept from an influential 1984 HBR paper by Hirotaka Takeuchi and Ikujiro Nonaka, titled "The new new product development game." The paper was a call to abandon the old and sequential product development approach, which the authors likened to a relay race, in favor of a new approach where the whole team moves forward as one, like a rugby scrum formation does.[8] Sutherland and Schwaber were honoring that rugby imagery when they named their methodology as Scrum.[6] They wanted the software world to abandon the sequential Waterfall approaches and deliver a working software product in each iteration.

Takeuchi and Nonaka paper was based on an analysis of a handful of Japanese companies—Fuji Xerox, Canon, Honda, and NEC—to curate their new product development principles. But their paper wasn't the only source of ideas for the Agile movement.

There was something else afoot in the 1980s. Everyone in the business world had a general curiosity why the Japanese were dominating so many manufacturing segments. To study the phenomena, MIT did a five-year research to analyze Japanese manufacturing systems, Toyota Production System (TPS) in particular, that concluded in 1991. They defined a term "lean" to label the core idea behind TPS—to improve productivity by eliminating unnecessary activities. It emphasized continuous improvement based on a framework consisting of *muri* (unreasonable overburdening), *mura* (reducing inconsistent workflows), and *muda* (eliminating waste). The MIT research ended by creating a new domain of lean production or manufacturing, the concepts of which form the foundation of Agile methodologies, like Lean software development and Kanban, that weren't around in 2001.[6]

The Lean Agile methods also introduced a new concept, *pivot*, into the business lexicon. *Pivot* refers to rapidly reorienting a project or an initiative, software development or otherwise, in response to the new information about the customer and the marketplace. This concept of rapid reorientation is at the heart of the contemporary view of business agility. But this concept owes its origin to a military strategy known as *maneuver warfare* and within that to a decision-making concept known as the OODA (*Observe, Orient, Decide, and Act*) loop.[9]

Colonel John Boyd of the US Air Force developed the maneuver warfare ideas and OODA loop concept based on the German Blitzkrieg principles used in World War II. Following that, Chet Richards has provided an excellent discussion of maneuver warfare concepts applied to business environments in his book *Certain to Win*.

When Boyd reviewed TPS, he concluded that it was an implementation of principles he had associated with maneuver warfare.[10] After studying the discussion in Chet's book, I think that Agile development methodologies are an implementation of maneuver warfare principles in software development. Maneuver warfare focuses on speeding up the OODA loops of the humans within groups engaged in a battle. Agile software development is about speeding the OODA loops, more generally decision cycles, of teams of developers so that they create products that win in the marketplace.

To Boyd, the maneuver warfare principles, even though originating in the military context, were not militaristic at all. They were cultural and concerned with human behavior and decision making within groups under conditions of stress. Agile authors concluded something similar while drafting the Manifesto[3]:

> *So in the final analysis, the meteoric rise of interest in—and sometimes tremendous criticism of—Agile Methodologies is about the mushy stuff of values and culture.*

While making that statement, they pointed a finger at the biggest reason Agile transformations within enterprise software fail. The enterprise companies fidget a lot about the mechanics and purity of the Agile methods. But before they do that, they do very little about getting the "mushy stuff" of culture and values right.

Maneuver Warfare and the Philosophy of Business Agility

The Boydian framework for maneuver warfare has four principles, all of which help speed up the OODA loops ("decision cycles") of humans working as groups. Because they encapsulate the nuances of cultural substrate required for agility so beautifully,[11] I will review them first before I analyze what enterprise companies can change about their Agile practices.

1. *Mutual Trust*

   Trust is the critical ingredient for transforming a group of people into a *team*. It speeds up the decision cycles because it unlocks the implicit communication. When there is trust, not everything needs to be written, reviewed, and approved. But mutual trust can't be manufactured or injected into a team from outside. It builds up within a team from mutual experience, more so when the team navigates the difficult experiences together. In a war context, it could mean people getting out of "warm and safe foxholes to face bullets." In a business context, it could mean putting in 80-hour weeks to meet deadlines. From my career, the projects I remember most are the more difficult ones. Outside of the team, an organizational environment of trust is fashioned by how leaders engage with the teams. When they do that, as Richards explains, an easy way to destroy trust is by micromanaging. While many enterprise companies tout trust as an organization value, they seldom put it into practice as a core cultural value. Centralized business planning comes in the way of putting faith in the teams. When projects go south, they micromanage through plans, instead of trusting the people to figure the specifics under broad mission-oriented guidelines.

2. *Intuitive Knowledge*

Stephen Curry, the 2022 NBA Finals MVP, shoots around 2,000 shots a week. He shoots and makes his shots at a high percentage even in the slightest space that he gets from his defenders. He has such an intuitive feel for it that he can find an opportunity in offensive situations that other players will not.[12] This type of intuitive feel for shooting that Curry demonstrates on the basketball court comes from years of practice, experience of being in live game situations, and discipline. The equivalent of this intuitive feel within business is the intuitive knowledge within a team of the bigger picture of what they are solving and how. Such intuitive knowledge can be a "source of power" and, similar to mutual trust, opens up implicit communication and speeds up decision cycles of individuals and teams. Without intuitive knowledge, there is no way to avoid formal planning. In the context of software development, a fast system for development is an outcome of intuitive knowledge of the specific business problems that developers and teams possess, not a system of rote implementation of Agile methods.

3. *Mission*

The Manifesto for Agile Software Development prioritizes "working software over comprehensive documentation" and has a principle that places the faith in "self-organizing teams" for the best output. The avoidance of comprehensive documentation is only possible when the implicit communication between and to the teams is strong. Mutual trust and intuitive knowledge are necessary but not sufficient ingredients for implicit communication. But for the team to take the next step to *self-organize*, those two aren't enough. In addition, the leadership has to manage through missions instead of top-down plans.

The mission, as per maneuver warfare, doesn't mean vague statements; it means something very specific. It refers to a responsibility-oriented contract between the leadership and the teams. The leadership creates a challenging mission, but provides the team autonomy and resources to fulfill it. Before that though, the mission is negotiated in an environment of trust and with teams having an intuitive knowledge of the overall business strategy. Very often, the missions go wrong because the leadership creates the challenging vision but cannot resist the temptation to micromanage the team. Or the leadership fails to communicate the business objectives clearly. But in managing through missions, micromanaging simply isn't allowed.

4. *Focusing Device*

I struggled with the idea of retaining influence but ceding control (not micromanaging) in the earlier part of my career. How do you know the team is headed in the right direction if you are not specifying every detail? It seemed a very hard question. Most people who struggle, or have struggled, to cede control will identify with this question. It's important enough in business, but is critical in situations like a war. For this conundrum, the doctrine of maneuver warfare has a concept called a focusing device. Along with the missions, what is typically needed is an organizing idea that can focus the direction of the team while fulfilling the mission. A focusing device is not an yearly business plan, like the ones common in big enterprise environment. It is a clear business strategy. Does everyone within the company know what it takes to win in the marketplace that the company operates in? Do they know how their individual work contributes to their company winning in the marketplace?

These four principles adapted from maneuver warfare are proven to help a group to win in a military conflict. When applied to business environments, these principles are proven to help businesses win within a competitive marketplace and build products that customers want to buy, like Toyota did with TPS. That's because these principles speed up the decision cycles of the individuals within groups, of employees within teams. These principles create conditions where the people involved can be their most creative to solve the problems at hand. These principles empower teams to take action during the most decisive moments. It is efficient because teams can act without decisions being shuttled up and down the food chain in organizational hierarchies.

Like maneuver warfare principles, the Agile values and principles advocate building teams that operate on trust and intuitive knowledge, have customer focused missions, and build winning products. The methods came later. The Agile values that came before aimed to improve the decision cycles of the software developers and teams. Because when followed in their truest sense, they elevate software development to something more than a mere obedience of orders. They elevate software development to something more than just meeting requirements at the lowest cost possible. They transform software development teams into an engine to build software products that customers want. They transform software development into the "labor that builds capital."

The (Un-Agile) Vignettes of Enterprise Software

Despite the widespread adoption of Agile practices within enterprise, beyond some ritualistic symbolism, it hasn't made enterprise software development actually Agile.

Before Agile, we had Gantt charts. Now, we have Gantt charts with Scrum sprints superimposed on them—what I like to call Waterfall dressed as Agile. Some companies have learned to disguise their inability to meaningfully adopt Agile by branding what they do as hybrid Agile.[13] That is fine if it is done for the right reason, that is, it is fit for purpose for a non-complex domain project, or it is done while transitioning to Agile to allow for adequate window for change. But it is often done for the wrong reasons.

The management wants to hear that the development is Agile, even if the cultural substrate isn't Agile. So what you get in reality is the symbolism of Agile ceremonies without real agility. The cultural environment for doing Agile within enterprise can sometimes be so woefully inadequate that there can be no path to Agile.

Why is that? There are some structural reasons. Let's review some vignettes from enterprise software environments that demonstrate why real agility becomes well nigh impossible.

1. *"Us vs. Them" Dynamics That Undermine Mutual Trust.*

   Whenever I attend a State-of-Agile-focused conversation with enterprise software audiences, I find it interesting that it is always organized by IT people. During such conversation, the discussion invariably meanders to a common grievance: *"We don't get clear user requirements from the business."* I also have the pleasure to hear from the other side, the business people. They are more direct: *"We don't trust our IT to deliver this program."*

   This business-IT divide is the fundamental roadblock for making enterprise software projects Agile, not any deficiency in processes or methods. Why? The lack of mutual trust between business and IT means their communications have to be more explicit—elaborate reports and documentation reviewed in endless cycles of meetings. In a low-trust environment, the business stakeholders don't try to think about reimagining their business processes: what is possible to do differently with what is available, rather than copying what you have heard others see and do. In response, the IT stakeholders just document and try to meet business requirements as dictated by the business. They don't venture to suggest what is possible to do differently from the existing ways to create a differentiated solution. As a result, most enterprise software programs tend to become a translation of existing ways of business operations into new technologies. There is no scope for experimentation.

In recent times, a new job category has emerged, which exacerbates the problem even further—the one of IT-business partners. The people working in this role liaise between assigned business units and IT teams so that business needs are translated properly to the development teams.

If there is a "lost in translation" problem between two groups, I fail to understand how inserting more translation will help in solving the problem or help build the missing trust. The business-IT divide is not the only "us vs. them" that prevents the buildup of trust. The large digital transformation programs rely on external teams of consultants to perform the actual development work. Not only that brings another "us vs. them" dynamic; it can also be detrimental to the second pillar of culture for agility, that is, intuitive knowledge.

2. *External Teams Prevent Accumulation of Intuitive Knowledge.*

External teams of contractors and consultants can be integrated into the enterprise development to varying degrees of success for a complicated domain project, but never for the complex

111

domain ones, because the external teams are engaged into the project with different incentives. They are focused on "delivering" on their *statements of work* (SoWs) agreed upon during the most uncertain phase of the project. They are not incentivized to come up with the best or the most innovative answers for solving the client problems. That is why for complex domain problems, like software for customer differentiation as we learned from the Hertz-Accenture example, relying on external teams doesn't work as it is typically executed.

For complex domains, as we discussed before, the actual product is not the software. It is the intuitive knowledge the team accumulates when they solve the problem with software. That intuitive knowledge, doesn't matter how well documented it is, diminishes when those external teams leave after the project is complete.

As it is, most enterprise development teams aren't provided clear missions. They are given highly elaborate specs to deliver as per the plans crafted by the management. But even when missions may exist, it is impossible to make an external team to act out your mission. Only your employees will, if you can engender mutual trust and intuitive knowledge among them. External teams try, but the paranoia of missing the deadline or agreed scope eventually takes over. When the risk of shipping on time increases, they stop acting like missionaries, however much they are integrated, but like mercenaries trying everything at their disposal to finish the assigned job.[14]

As a result, it is extra hard to make insourced software development Agile. It doesn't matter what the intentions are, there simply isn't enough mutual trust and experience to create mission-based responsibility contracts that vest the control with the external teams. Without the mission-based vested responsibility, the enterprise company leadership wants the detailed status reports on progress or lack thereof. The status report becoming a measure of progress creates a perverse incentive: "looking good" gets priority over "doing the right thing."

There is only one way to avoid this incentive: by making working software as the only measure of progress. From my personal experience, I can attest that many practitioners of enterprise software would love to see that happen. But the reason it doesn't happen is an almost religious belief in the effectiveness of formal planning at the management level.

3. *Formal Planning Crowds Out the Innovative Pivots.*

    It is baffling to me how sacred we treat formal plans in enterprise software programs. On average, 70% of projects miss the plan in some dimension.[15] Yet, we try hard to conform to each one we create. Teams endure many unnatural contortions to preserve the sanctity of those plans. And, when plans go south, the consensus takeaway always is to make those plans even more sacred, that is, even more thorough and even more scientific planning.

    Over-optimism in plans goes beyond software. It is a human cognitive bias. The Nobel laureate Daniel Kahneman named it the Planning Fallacy. Per Kahneman, we over-index on the causal role of our skills and things we control. We ignore causal interactions from outside the project and existential reality we don't control.[16]

    A project deadline based on an estimate done during the most uncertain phase of the project is an extreme example of the Planning Fallacy (Figure 5-1). Making a deadline sacred such that it can't be missed at any cost should count as a form of self-flagellation, because team incentives stem from the risks the leadership prioritizes. Fear of an arbitrary deadline (risk of shipping on time) drawn in advance duly tramples over any chance for creating a creative environment to build software and create great products for customers (risk of shipping the right thing).

A long plan to deliver fixed and predetermined scope comes in the way of using software to discover and build value. There is a trajectory to software evolution in the XaaS era. Commodity technology becomes reusable open source software (e.g., JavaScript frameworks, ML frameworks). Templates become products to buy (e.g., cloud app ecosystems). Products become services to rent (e.g., cloud services). With ever-increasing options to reuse, buy, and rent, there is little to no value in merely implementing those options, as we noted in the Shift Principle. The value comes from remixing those options to create new recipes for differentiated customer value.

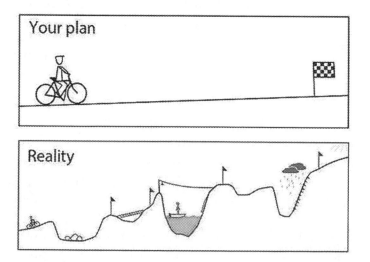

Figure 5-1. *Planning Fallacy (Source: Twitter/@dinapomeranz)*

The mechanism for creating new software recipes is iterating with "working software"—putting the *MSS* (assembled as much as possible from commercial software) in front of the customers and users and fixing the incongruities they face iteratively and continuously. Agile authors laid down a clear principle: "working software is the primary measure of progress," because it is only the "working software" that uncovers innovative possibilities that planning can't identify. Staying flexible on what you will ship in three to six months prevents underestimating what is possible in the long term, because the clear next step to ship "working software" in the next two to four weeks prevents overestimating what is possible in the short term. Operating from "working software," in some way, is like learning to walk in the fog. We plan for what we can see. Once you execute that plan, more of the path shows up. That allows planning for that next course.

However, implementing "working software" as a measure of progress is easier said than done in the enterprise environment. Without the cultural substrate encapsulated within the maneuver warfare principle—one with trust, intuitive knowledge, mission, and focus—it is impossible. You will never walk in the fog with someone you don't trust or whose knowledge you don't respect. Neither will you if you don't know your mission for walking in the uncertainty of fog.

4. *Meeting Requirements Rules Out Winning Products.*

The next stumbling block with Agile in enterprise is the customer requirements, or rather their source. In other words, where do the business requirements come from? Whether it is an internal customer, a business user, or an actual customer, the idea that they know what a business requirement should be is wrong.

Chet Richards touches upon this idea as follows:

Customers often want things because competitors have dan-gled them in their faces. In either case, such "discovery of cus-tomer wants" does not provide the basis for strategy; it represents a failure of strategy.

Chet notes that discovering customer "wants" may not generate much in the way of useful strategy because what customers often want is magic—something like IBM's "server pixie dust" in their 2003 commercials or unlimited free energy or instant cures of pains and aches, with no side effects.[17]

That is what I observe sometimes when engaging with customers. The most sought-after things are often the shiniest things. These are things embedded in marketing campaigns at the glitzy tech conferences that keep glitzier by the day. There is nary a thought about specific customer problems, but a lot of desire for high-level technological transformation. The want begins and ends with fancy things that new technology allows.

Meeting business requirements without the associated diligence of specific customer problems can never create unique value, as we learned with the Value Principle. The requirements for a winning product have to be rooted in strategy to win in the marketplace, through products that external customers must buy or that internal customers must use. The product has to create progress for the customer that can be validated.

The preceding fallacy is a specific case of mistaking strategic planning for a business strategy. Executing plans for meeting business requirements at the lowest cost possible is still popular because it is comfortable. Such plans deal with the cost side of the resources, and controlling costs is easier than achieving a business outcome that is uncertain and uncontrollable. Therefore, it is important to internalize the difference between a plan and a strategy.

Roger Martin, a business professor at the University of Toronto, has an excellent definition for strategy[18]:

> *A strategy is an integrative set of choices that*
> *positions you on a playing field of your choice in a*
> *way that you win.*

Applying Martin's definition, software development driven by a strategy must have a hypothesis on why adopting some shiny technology will result in progress for the enterprise's internal or external customers. Seen that way, a strategy can act like a *focusing device*. Without such a strategy, most development projects end up as either translating existing ways of working into newer technologies or imitating what others are doing with similar technologies in the marketplace.

How to Implement a Strategy of Agility (Powered by Software)

In my conversations, executives at enterprise companies often describe agility as an expectation to move fast. What they typically mean is having an ability to deliver projects fast. But that can't happen by just asking developers to adopt Agile methods. A truly Agile delivery of software can only happen in an enterprise that leverages agility as a foundation for business strategy.

"A strategy of agility" that Chet Richards describes isn't about moving fast at all. It isn't even about responding to change fast. It is about "shaping the marketplace" on your terms by creating winning products. Such a strategy has to lead the enterprise company "and its customer into new ways of conceiving their product or service."[19] I am going to take this concept of agility and explore it in the context of software development, because creating winning software products, or developing enterprise software for innovative use cases.

117

Beyond an implementation of Agile methods, what does a whole strategy of agility powered by software look like? The enterprise management must reconfigure specific operational elements of software development

1. *Create Small Autonomous Teams.*

    A team is a fundamental unit for software engineering work, not a resource, not person hours or days. That was the enduring finding from the Takeuchi and Nonaka paper and from MIT's research on TPS. And that is what even Sutherland and Schwaber recommended with Scrum principles. A team is most granular organizational element to build *mutual trust* and *intuitive knowledge,* for increasing implicit communications, that can then propagate within the organization. For this concept of a team, it is almost an imperative that business and technical stakeholders accountable for the software deliverable exist within the same team to avoid the "us vs. them."

    How *small* should such a team be? There is no hard rule. One key thing to note is that the communication overhead increases exponentially as the number of team members increase. It becomes impossible to make communications implicit in a 50-person team. Hence, heuristics like the Bezos Two-Pizza Rule can be useful. The size of the best-performing teams in my portfolio hovers around eight to ten. It is a size at which, I have come to believe, most of the communications can stay implicit, once that sized group has had the mutual experience of working together.

    Each such team should have a customer—internal or external. Proximity to their customers (not physical but mental), and the opportunity to solve their problems, is what motivates people within a team. That should become their *mission*. What helps their customer to make progress should act as the *focusing device*.

Each such team should have a single leader—no two-in-a-box, no dotted lines. Within the context of what the team does, this leader along with their team must be empowered to make every decision that helps their team solve customer problems. That brings us around to the second condition around this team—it must be *autonomous*. Most companies tout empowerment, but rarely vest the real decision-making control, because plan-driven environments, still highly prevalent, never allow enough psychological safety for decentralized decision making at a team level. Therefore, there has to be a different alternative to managing than a plan.

2. *Manage Teams Through Responsibility Contracts (a.k.a. "No Micromanaging").*

The biggest danger to mutual trust is micromanaging, as Chet Richards explains. Even at a personal level, the biggest hurdle for me to transition from an individual contributor to a leader of teams was giving up control. When things go south, and there is difficulty to meet a prescribed plan, there is an irresistible temptation to take control. Instead, the management has to learn to cede control to small teams but still retain influence.

Chet Richards describes an idea called "contract of leadership," adapted from maneuver warfare. The leader's job is not to micromanage through a top-down plan, but communicate responsibility through a clear mission. When viewed as a two-way contract, leadership isn't delegating tasks and getting status reports back. It is assigning a challenging problem to the team and getting "a continuous flow of information about the unfolding situation" back. This flow of information is not to suss out whether the team is doing exactly what you have asked them (characteristic of low-trust management). Instead, it is to know when to "adjust and modify" the assigned challenge, as soon as the need arises.

I must emphasize that the word *contract* here doesn't imply something legal. It means a mutual mechanism to "discover understanding and foster responsibility" between leadership and teams and across teams. Contracts can be a great way of improving communications between teams in a large development program or an organization.

Jeff Lawson provides a great example of this idea at Amazon and Twilio. Each team has a charter that describes "what we do, how can you engage with us."[20] Teams implement those contracts in software code, as a now widely understood architecture pattern known as "microservice." This is a highly applicable concept when enterprise companies have to bring external teams. Such teams should be bringing or building their own working software and engaging with internal teams building software through responsibility contracts, preferably implemented through a software-driven interface or an API. Each team, internal or external, should have a software deliverable and must have a published interface to engage for other teams.

3. *Install "Working Software" as a Measure of Progress.*

An aspect of managing through contracts in software development—assessing "the flow of information about the unfolding situation" to "adjust and modify"—is seeing the working software often and consistently. It is ten times more efficient a sensing tool than color-coded statuses on a PowerPoint slide. If just seeing doesn't feel enough, a leader and a manager should check it out as a user, for each iteration. Yes, not everyone can write code, but everyone knows how to log into a software system.

In larger enterprise software programs, there is an incredible amount of wasteful management overhead due to status reporting. Jason Fried and David Heinemeier Hansson write about it eloquently in their book *Rework*[21]:

The business world is littered with dead documents that do nothing but waste people's time. Reports no one reads, diagrams no one looks at, and specs that never resemble the finished product. These things take forever to make but only seconds to forget.

I have been on enterprise software projects where we had to create such "dead documents" several times during a single week. It was reviewed by a layer of management on the side of my leadership and another layer on the client side, before it was reported to the executives. After the meetings, these documents were filed away and promptly forgotten. And the project management teams started preparing for the next meeting coming up. In an environment like that, the progress on the actual project, the true sense of which is only apparent to the developers, is liable to get lost in translation. In response to subjective statuses on a report, the focus shifts to "messaging" to avoid causing panic rather than rapidly adjusting to "an unfolding situation." As Richards also calls out[22]

Rather than quick decision cycles about things important to customers, the focus of the company's efforts turn to internal politics and creative justification.

"Looking good" takes precedence over adjusting and modifying for real project progress. The antidote for valueless work, like status reporting, as Fried and Heinemeier Hansson suggest, is to "get real." Nothing helps more in getting real on the project progress than looking at the working software system and assessing progress risks.

The real agility comes from eliminating wasteful activities. Shedding cumbersome status reporting in favor of assessing real progress through working software is a potent way of doing that.

4.   *Deliver on the Reciprocal Obligations to the Teams.*

Over-customizing packaged software is a terrible idea because it increases the overall system cost. But an even bigger ill effect is that it undermines the most significant tenet of the strategy of agility.

It prevents the enterprise company from leveraging "time as a shaping mechanism" for creating emergent value, the one that can't be planned for but only discovered through applying software to business problems iteratively. Instead of making good RBRB micro-decisions to create a dynamic software stack, such that they can iterate rapidly with customers, the companies end up recreating old systems with new technologies.

For new innovation, they should be building from requirements rooted in a business strategy to create winning products. The business professor Roger Martin reminds the following about strategy[18]:

A strategy specifies an outcome, a competitive outcome that you wish to achieve, which involves customers wanting your product or service, that they will buy enough of it, to make the profitability that you'd like to make. The tricky thing about that is that you don't control them. You might wish you could, but you can't. They decide, not you. That's a harder trick.

> Only the internal or external customer decides whether your software product is valuable, as we noted in the Value Principle. As an enterprise company, you need to have a hypothesis of why that would be. To create a fitting solution, you have to empower your teams to iterate from customer feedback. The management responsibility, instead of micromanaging, is to create the stack to build the *most simple system* (MSS) quickly, so that teams can start iterating without delay.

The new value doesn't stem from technology. It is created by the small autonomous teams solving customer problems the right way. It comes from the output of the small autonomous teams operating at the top of their creative license. That is the enduring insight of the principles of maneuver warfare, which generated success with TPS for Toyota, and what the founders of Scrum put at the core of their methodology. It is what Agile authors wished for when they concluded that Agile is about "mushy stuff" of the organizational culture that unlocks creative work.

As a result, the real imperative for executives and leaders isn't to micromanage adoption of an Agile methodology like Scrum. It is to meet their reverse obligation to make the teams Agile: by creating a culture for teams to operate at their most creative self, by providing them the dynamic software stack so that these teams can iterate for their customers quickly, and by managing through two-way responsibility contracts built on mutual trust and knowledge.

Agile Culture Begets (Rapid) Flow of Value

Over the last decade and a half, the world has woken up to the value of business agility even beyond software. For example, one of the performance criteria I have to self-assess at my current employer is my business agility. I think, in general, this is a good development. The more the business stakeholders or, as Fowler would call them, "the nontechnical people" try to practice Agile, the more they will learn the inadequacy of the ways in which they are trying to make "the technical people" Agile.

Doesn't matter the methodology you employ, whether it is Scrum, Kanban, or some Lean method; it is impossible to become Agile without the cultural values for its proper underpinning, because the main objective can't be some ritualistic adherence to methodological artifacts of Scrum. It has to be to create a cultural environment where every employee can be at their most creative self. As the Agile authors reminded us, the objective has to be always to create such an environment [3]

> *… that does more than talk about "people as our most important asset" but actually "acts" as if people were the most important, and lose the word "asset."*

Even though the values espoused in the Agile Manifesto are spot on, they can seem a bit arbitrary to anyone who is not steeped in the history of Agile— "mushy" and unwieldy. That is why I believe it is critical to bring a study of maneuver warfare principles in business (beautifully explained by Chet Richards) and introduce them into the discussion of enterprise Agile. Yes, you need a methodology to make the practice real when you are starting out, but as a management team, you need to do the required work to make mutual trust and intuitive knowledge the fundamental values of your organizational culture first. You have to review and fine-tune your internal communications to evaluate if they encapsulate your mission and strategic focus adequately. Software development can't be Agile in a business that isn't Agile.

It is unequivocally true that software can be a source of business agility. As we discussed with the Shift Principle, software can be a paradigm of innovation. But the aforementioned is true only in an organizational environment where software developers, and teams of software developers, can practice creatively. That is what the review of maneuver warfare principles signifies; that is what a more in-depth review of Agile Manifesto reveals. Under conditions of uncertainty, the most critical thing for making fast progress is how quick the decision cycles are of the people involved and how much of the communication around those decisions can be implicit—within a team, between teams and management, and among the teams. While methodologies can help in formalizing behaviors of Agile practice, they won't yield anything without the Agile culture, without the "mushy stuff" of Agile values.

The Agile Manifesto, even though it was predated by methodologies like Scrum, never recommended a methodology. It never recommended a specific tool to manage the Agile processes, even though there are a ton of tools in the market now to do so. It simply outlined organizational values and principles to achieve agility. The real issue now is that Agile has become all about processes and tools, while we have forgotten about those values and principles.

We need to correct the imbalance.

While there is value in following Agile processes and tools, we have to value the cultural aspect of Agile more. Because doing that guarantees the flow of business value from software that is the cherished goal of every enterprise business in the Age of Software.

The Culture Principle   Agile software development happens only in an Agile business culture. Therefore, implement your strategy of business agility before you implement Agile development methods.

Key Tenets:

- Agile methodologies are widely adopted. But despite the widespread use, there is discontent around the actual benefits of Agile customer-focused innovation.

- Agile was drafted to focus on organizational values centered on culture. The state of the practice has become all about the methods, while the core values are forgotten.

- The core ideas of Agile trace back to World War II understood as maneuver warfare principles. The ideas are about making groups of people effective when facing conditions of uncertainty and stress. They are

    - Mutual trust

    - Intuitive knowledge

    - Mission orientation

    - Focus in direction

- After World War II, these ideas were successfully implemented in lean manufacturing, most notably by Toyota in their Toyota Production System. The same ideas are foundational to the Agile Manifesto.

- But Agile as currently implemented in enterprise software conflicts with these ideas.

- Therefore, real agility can't be about methods. But it has to be understood and practiced as a business strategy powered by software innovation. The following are the components of a strategy of agility.

- **Create Small Autonomous Teams**: These teams are units of engineering to build trust and intuitive knowledge.

- **Manage Teams Through Responsibility Contracts**: Communicate missions to the teams as responsibility. Don't assign specs but problems to solve.

- **Install "Working Software" as a Measure of Progress**: Review and adjust based on the progress understood from working software and customer feedback.

- **Deliver on the Reciprocal Obligations to the Teams**: The management shouldn't micromanage, but reciprocate on their obligations for agility—creating a dynamic stack for iteration and creating a creative culture.

- There is value in following Agile processes and tools, but we have to value the cultural aspect of Agile more.

- Doing that guarantees the flow of business value from software that is the cherished goal of every enterprise business in the Age of Software.

References

[1]   Nyce, C. M. (2017, December 8). *The Winter Getaway That Turned the Software World Upside Down*. The Atlantic. Retrieved September 20, 2022, from www.theatlantic.com/technology/archive/2017/12/agile-manifesto-a-history/547715/

[2]   Agile Alliance. (2001). *Manifesto for Agile Software Development*. Manifesto for Agile Software Development. https://agilemanifesto.org/

[3]   Agile Alliance. (2001). *History: The Agile Manifesto*. Manifesto for Agile Software Development. https://agilemanifesto.org/history.html

[4]   Hunter, T. (2020, August 18). *Kent Beck Says Tech Has a Compassion Problem*. Built In. Retrieved March 20, 2021, from https://builtin.com/software-engineering-perspectives/kent-beck-geeks-gusto-globalization

[5]   Fowler, M. (2018, August 25). *The State of Agile Software in 2018*. Martin Fowler. Retrieved March 20, 2022, from https://martinfowler.com/articles/agile-aus-2018.html

[6]   Rigby, D., Sutherland, J., & Takeuchi, H. (2016, April 20). *The Secret History of Agile Innovation*. Harvard Business Review. Retrieved April 20, 2022, from https://hbr.org/2016/04/the-secret-history-of-agile-innovation

[7]   Preiss, K., Goldman, S. L., & Nagel, R. N. (1994). *Agile Competitors and Virtual Organizations: Strategies for Enriching the Customer*. Wiley.

[8]   Takeuchi, H., & Nonaka, I. (1986, January). *The New New Product Development Game*. Harvard Business Review. Retrieved April 20, 2022, from https://hbr.org/1986/01/the-new-new-product-development-game

[9] Rao, V. (2018, February 8). *Rough Consensus and Maximal Interestingness*. Breaking Smart. https://breakingsmart.com/en/season-1/rough-consensus-and-maximal-interestingness/

[10] Richards, C. (2004). *Certain to Win: The Strategy of John Boyd, Applied to Business* (Kindle ed., page 5). Xlibris.

[11] Richards, C. (2004). *Certain to Win: The Strategy of John Boyd, Applied to Business* (Kindle ed., Chapter 5). Xlibris.

[12] Jenkins, S. (2016, April 8). *The hidden price Steph Curry pays for making the impossible seem effortless*. The Washington Post. www.washingtonpost.com/sports/wizards/steph-curry-can-he-handle-the-full-court-pressure-of-super-stardom/2016/04/08/3dc96ca8-f6ab-11e5-a3ce-f06b5ba21f33_story.html

[13] Hartman, B., Griffiths, M., Rothman, J., Fewell, J., Kauffman, B., Matola, S., & Slusanschi, H. (2017, January 4). *What Is Hybrid Agile, Anyway?* Agile Alliance. www.agilealliance.org/what-is-hybrid-agile-anyway/

[14] Wharton School of Business. (2000, April 13). *Mercenaries vs. Missionaries: John Doerr Sees Two Kinds of Internet Entrepreneurs*. Knowledge at Wharton. https://knowledge.wharton.upenn.edu/article/mercenaries-vs-missionaries-john-doerr-sees-two-kinds-of-internet-entrepreneurs/

[15] Portman, H. (2021, January 6). *Review Standish Group—CHAOS 2020: Beyond Infinity | Henny Portman's Blog*. Henny Portman. https://hennyportman.wordpress.com/2021/01/06/review-standish-group-chaos-2020-beyond-infinity/

[16] Kahneman, D. (2013). *Thinking, Fast and Slow* (page 249). Farrar, Straus and Giroux.

[17]   Richards, C. (2004). *Certain to Win: The Strategy of John Boyd, Applied to Business* (Kindle ed., page 68). Xlibris.

[18]   Harvard Business Review. (2022, June 29). *A Plan Is Not a Strategy*. YouTube. Retrieved August 18, 2022, from `https://youtu.be/iuYlGRnC7J8`

[19]   Richards, C. (2004). *Certain to Win: The Strategy of John Boyd, Applied to Business* (Kindle ed., page 57). Xlibris.

[20]   Lawson, J. (2021). *Ask Your Developer: How to Harness the Power of Software Developers and Win in the 21st Century* (Kindle ed., page 192). Harper Business.

[21]   Fried, J., & Hansson, D. H. (2010). *Rework* (Kindle ed., loc. 632). Crown Business.

[22]   Richards, C. (2004). *Certain to Win: The Strategy of John Boyd, Applied to Business* (Kindle ed., page 57). Xlibris.

CHAPTER 6

Manage Development Flow, Not Project or Product

The Flow Principle

What should we change in our product development process? Eliminate waste? Increase quality? Raise efficiency? Shorten cycle time? The key to answering this question is to step back to a more basic question: Why do we want to change the product development process? The answer: to increase profits.

—Donald G. Reinertsen

Systems of information-feedback control are fundamental to all life and human endeavor, from the slow pace of biological evolution to the launching of latest space satellite… Everything we do as individuals, as an industry, or as a society is done in the context of an information-feedback system.

—Jay W. Forrester

The problem is not with our organizations realizing that they need to transform; the problem is that organizations are using managerial frameworks and infrastructure models from past revolutions to manage their businesses in this one.

—Mik Kersten

The real deliverable of software development work isn't a project or a product. It is to create business value that is repeatable and predictable.

As it used to happen during *digitization* and *digitalization* eras, implementation and massive customization of commercial enterprise software packages doesn't create value anymore. The business value is created through new and differentiated solutions for internal and external customers, through innovative and novel use cases of software.

The tried and tested approach of transforming existing IT operations with new software has outlived its utility. When every enterprise is implementing the same software, new and differentiated value comes from business innovation you can create with deployed software: from finding new ways to serve and delight customers, from discovering new business models around products or services, and from improving employee and customer experience.

While new technologies enable that, the real engine to discover and build new value is the creative work of human talent. The Culture Principle requires that an enterprise *must* create an environment where their developers and teams can be their most creative. But aspects like creativity and empowerment are difficult to get right. They fall into this fuzzy realm of values and culture—easy to vouch for, but extremely hard to implement. And when the business isn't doing well, just when the organization needs it the most, the kind of decentralized decision making that makes creative work thrive becomes the most scarce.

But even when business times aren't tough, the track record of enterprise software to create repeatable and predictable new business value is abysmal. While the consumer and sell side of enterprise software companies are amassing outsized financial value, the enterprises are stuck spinning on endless spending cycles hitched on to the digital transformation bandwagon. To get off this unending spin cycle, I believe we require something different to translate the remarkable potential of modern software into repeatable and predictable enterprise business value.

We certainly don't need more methods. While methods are helpful, the cottage industries that tend to develop around them obscure their actionable knowledge. More than any new method, we have to strip away some of the complexity that has accumulated around our methods. What we actually need is to *relearn* the constituting elements of Agile software development. We have to stop retrofitting old ways of software management into Agile methodologies. What we actually need is to *reorient* back to managing the flow of business value through software development.

Software Development Lifecycle and Business Value

For an enterprise company, the business value from software can accrue in a couple of ways. From an external customer, it can accrue through a standalone product or service or as a digital companion to other enterprise products or services. From internal customers, it's when their use of the solution increases the operational efficiency.

Let us associate this business value to the software development lifecycle (SDLC). As we know from the Value Principle, the real source of value comes from creating customer progress. The specific ideas that can help customers make progress, typically referred to as business requirements, are inputs to the SDLC. A working software solution that results in real customer progress is an output of the SDLC.

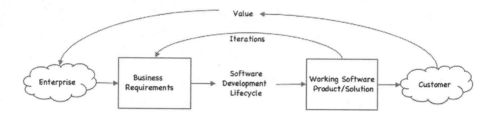

Figure 6-1. *SDLC flow and business value*

Translating a hypothetical new idea into tangible financial value isn't a straight line. It requires a certain amount of trial and error, many iterations within the lifecycle. Even though enterprise planning assumes it so, it is never a "get it right in one go" big transformation project or some preconceived notion of a customer product or service. It takes many cycles of continuous improvement to create value. Ergo, the end objective can't be achieving state-of-the-art product management or project management competencies. It is achieving the optimal flow of work and information within this SDLC that maximizes business value.

This nuance, while I would like to think is decently understood, is at least hopelessly lost among the prevalent management practices within enterprise software. I see enterprise IT departments hiring trained product owners or product managers in droves because they want to transition from executing projects to building products. I often see project management folks dressing industrial ways of software management as hybrid Agile. But I rarely see an honest and sincere discussion about maximizing the flow of tangible business value from the SDLC.

To correct that, the focus must shift from *delivery-based* management to *flow-based* management within enterprise software. We have to stop searching for methodological silver bullets. Instead, we must find an answer to a more pertinent, more interesting, and a far more meatier software management question:

How can each team achieve the optimal development flow unique to its context that includes its customer, the specific problem it is solving, and the tools it is using to solve the problem?

Know Thy Queues First

Nothing illustrates optimizing flow better than management of traffic flow.

On busy freeways during the rush hour, ramp meters control the pace at which new vehicles merge onto the freeway. Ramp meters, placed at the beginning of the on-ramp, stop the vehicle with a red light. After some elapsed time, the vehicle is green-lighted onto the freeway. The time between red and green lights is controlled by a computer that adjusts the timing based on the current traffic conditions on the freeway. This small constraint on new vehicles is proven to maintain a better traffic flow, especially during crowded hours.

A ramp meter is a device for managing traffic queues. And queue management is the most fundamental problem of operations management. Examples of queues being managed (or mismanaged) are everywhere in daily life: traffic lights at intersections, airport security lines, hospital emergency rooms, restaurant wait queues on weekend nights, and all other countless lines we wait in while going about our lives.

The goal of queue management is to minimize the delay, because associated with delay, there is often a financial, an economic, or a human cost. Restaurants can lose their customers. Commuting delays can be a drag on human productivity (and economic productivity) when people waste their time commuting. When global supply chains got backlogged during the pandemic, it resulted in an economic cost in the form of inflation.

Thankfully, we have the queuing theory to help with answers to queue management problems. The queuing theory originated in the early 1900s to understand and analyze the flow of calls through telephone exchanges. Agner Krarup Erlang's work at Copenhagen Telephone Company, to predict when a call would be blocked (given a specific phone line capacity utilization),[1] was so effective that the principles of the theory have since been applied to a wide range of fields like transportation, manufacturing, and services delivery. Yet, for an unfathomable reason, it is missing in the field of software development.

Like what Erlang was dealing with phone call traffic, software development work has similar challenges. Enterprise software programs start with a long queue, a long list of business requirements. Most of these requirements require a level of scrubbing to determine the actual work content. Even after such scrubbing, these requirements can change in unpredictable ways and at unpredictable times after the work starts. The higher the degree of innovation, the higher the frequency of such change requests. The forecast error on delivering this work can be large and can get larger after the work starts. But we have to deliver this work on a predictable timeline, and it is expected to create tangible value.

Just like there are queues everywhere in daily life, there are queues in software development. A long list of initial requirements is just one example. The ongoing work within each development iteration is another one. So are completed code waiting on testers and work waiting on a single unicorn developer in whose absence everything falls apart.

The management is trained to keep a hawk-like eye on how development is tracking as compared with the forecast. But I have seldom come across any manager who is curious about where such queues are forming and what can be done to resolve them. The management has to switch to keeping a hawk-like eye for where development work is piling up in queues.

136

Managing flow is managing queues.[2] The most optimal flow happens when long queues are avoided. The prime concern of flow-based software management isn't timelines or budgets against the forecasts. It focuses on variables that maximize the flow of value.

(Long) Queues Hinder the Flow of Value

If you have ever observed an artist draw, you will notice that they will zoom out every so often and observe the canvas. Occasionally, they're maybe admiring their work. But mostly they are observing their feedback.

Every creative work—painting, drawing, writing, or music—improves through feedback. For a hobbyist, it is easier because all they have to do is take a step back and take a critical look. It gets harder when you have to create things for commercial value. Stand-up artists practice their punchlines in comedy clubs, before they settle on the ones to use in their Netflix special. It becomes even harder when groups of people are creating new things. In addition to getting feedback, groups have to jell together and build mutual experience. Theater productions go through rehearsal performances in low-stake environments, before they go live on Broadway. Getting and incorporating feedback is the currency to add value to creative work.

Building new and differentiated customer value with software, a must within the Age of Software, is creative work. Like theater productions and stand-up artists, the developing teams need to get and incorporate rounds of feedback from their customers—internal or external. Shortening this feedback cycle accelerates value because teams can understand whether the built solution fits the customer's needs faster.

Rapid customer feedback provides information to abandon development paths of low value.[3] It also provides insights into paths of emergent customer value not previously understood. This is what the Agile Manifesto is also alluding to when it urges[4]

Welcome changing requirements, even late in development.

Changing requirements represent a feedback loop on what may be valuable to customers. The Manifesto immediately goes on to offer another suggestion[4]:

Deliver working software frequently, from a couple of weeks to a couple of months, with a preference to the shorter timescale.

The *shorter timescale* enables faster feedback, which is critical to iterative software development. But when change requests get stuck in a long queue, it hampers this iterative process of refining the software solution in collaboration with the customer. The prevailing dogma of enterprise software management is that an adequate response to a long queue is to add capacity (new developers) or to increase utilization of existing capacity (asking developers to work nights and weekends). That's because it is easier for the management to understand the cost of capacity than the cost of delayed work.[5] In the absence of the latter, the management tries to be as efficient as possible with the former.

But we know more developers increase the communication overhead within the team. Each new developer needs time to build mutual trust and experience before they become effective within the team. Even if you can accommodate that, additional capacity can only resolve a long queue state for work that is noncritical. And higher capacity utilization just worsens the long queue, because when capacity is at or above 100% utilization, there is none left to intake a new or a changing requirement. The new requirement just gets added to the queue. It doesn't require too much cleverness to understand that any work at the end of the queue is going to take longer to get done than the work at the beginning.[6] As a result, the cycle time of each new or changed requirement gets longer. That is why programs that start with a large list of requirements end up with a list of pending requirements even larger.

At the heart of this dogma, there is an erroneous assumption that software development work can be managed like other industrial processes. But as we analyzed in the Complexity Principle, software development is a complex system of entities—people (developers, management, customers), software system, and business requirements— interconnected in ways that it is impossible to predict and control its behavior. You can't manage that linearly through tracking timelines and budgets. Instead, you need a management framework that embraces the complexity of various information loops that come from the interconnections. That is where flow-based management approach comes in. Instead of managing people or business requirements or forecasts, it focuses on optimizing the information flow within the software development lifecycle.

The Levers for Optimizing Flow

A complex system is best understood as a combination of stocks and flows. Stocks represent the system structure—a store, a quantity, or any accumulation of material or information. Flows represent the system behavior. Stocks change through actions of flows.[7] During a rush hour, the total number of vehicles on a congested stretch of the freeway is a stock. Vehicles entering and exiting that stretch are the inflow and outflow, respectively.

If inflow is higher than outflow, the traffic congestion increases. If the outflow is higher than the inflow, the congestion decreases. While flows control the dynamics of a stock, they are harder to observe than the stocks. It is easier to see the traffic but much harder to see how vehicle inflow and outflow are impacting the changing traffic. One other dynamic to understand is that stocks have inherent momentum. Traffic congestion takes time to build, and after it builds up, it takes time to ebb away. The larger the stock, the larger the momentum of stock changes in any direction.

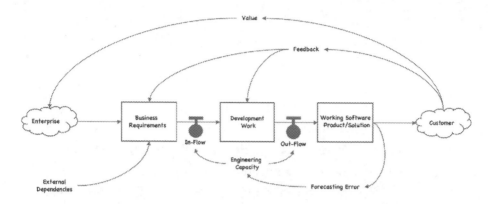

Figure 6-2. *Feedback loops within software development*

We can leverage this same model of stocks and flows for a software development program. Business requirements, a store of accumulated information about customer needs, are a stock. You need to expend some engineering effort to translate those requirements into actual development work (documented as user stories), also a store of accumulated information about what should be built as a solution. Further engineering work converts that stock into a working software solution that customers can see and interact with. The prevailing management paradigm pays a lot of attention to requirements and user stories (the stocks)—to build forecasts for estimated timelines and budgets and to track actual progress compared with forecasts. It pays very little attention to the behavior and efficiency of the various flows (represented as arrows in Figure 6-2).

I am proposing that we fix our attention deficit to these flows to create enterprise software of repeatable and predictable business value. Our core objective must be to shorten the customer feedback cycle, which is a source of value. We want to get customer feedback on our solution hypothesis as early and as often as we can.

I have learned the core ideas that I am recommending from studying Donald Reinertsen's work as discussed in his book *The Principles of Product Development Flow*. Donald's work is vast and is a must-read for any practitioner involved in new product development of any kind.

I have attempted to learn from Donald's work and adapt the core ideas to enterprise software development. I am suggesting five concepts in the following to improve the enterprise software development flow:

1. *Reduce Your Batch Size.*[8]

    Tourist towns love tourists, except the ones that arrive on a cruise ship for a day, because a large batch of cruise ship tourists damages the flow of tourist activities within such towns. A local restaurant can handle a steady stream of customers in groups of three or four, but gets crushed when 50–60 people who have just disembarked from a cruise ship show up.

    Like these tourist towns discover, work in large batch sizes is detrimental to a good operational flow. Similarly, if you start your software development project with a large list of requirements (i.e., large batch size), you can forget about achieving flow within your development. For that matter, you can even stop worrying about being responsive to changing requirements. An oil tanker takes a lot longer to turn around in open water than a small speedboat. As we discussed earlier, large stocks have big momentum, and their flows take longer to adjust. A smaller queue of work (i.e., small batch size) simply clears quicker than a larger one, resulting in a short cycle time. Shorter cycle times mean there is a lower cost of delay for work items waiting to get into the queue next.

    Therefore, working in small batches increases the frequency of customer feedback. When building software solutions of new and differentiated value, we have to try new things and run the risk of failure. A failure in a small batch is economically more efficient than a failure in a large batch. A small failure can even be viewed as a cost for new information about customer preferences. In that sense, developing in small batches reduces the overall risk of a development program. And it focuses on the pursuit of efficiency at the right place, the financial outcomes of software development, instead of pursuing efficiency in capacity utilization or managing to forecast.

Rapid feedback increases the sense of responsibility for the development teams. If I am working on a single piece of software that needs to be demonstrated to the end customer in five days, I am fully engaged. If I have hundreds of such pieces to work on and my immediate coding deliverable isn't due for months, there is a high probability that procrastination will set in. Furthermore, the best way to energize the developers is reducing the cycle time for meaningful feedback on their work product. And small batches are the best way to accomplish that.

What is the optimal size for a batch? The right answer is whatever makes sense for a given team. For example, a batch that could be executed in two weeks turned out to be the most optimal for my teams. When I started with these teams, we were at a batch size of four months. We gradually brought down our batch size, to shave off cycle time one week at a time. After testing many configurations, a batch executable in two weeks turned out to be the best for us. But we build B2B software solutions that have some regulatory compliance requirements. So while a two-week batch size may work for us, it may not work for an enterprise building B2C solutions. In such cases, a batch size may need further reduction such that it can be executed in a few hours or a day.

You might be wondering why I am describing the batch sizes in time and not in ubiquitously used story points. It is because story points are meant to attribute complexity to a particular user story, not to be used as an estimation variable. When it comes to estimation, any developer can better estimate what they can do in one to two days than what they will do in several weeks. Each user story should be broken down until it is small enough to be completed in one to two days. It is far easier to plan your batch with user stories defined like that than using story points.

Even after your best attempt to reduce the batch size, if it is still taking you more than a month to execute a cycle, you must take a closer look at work within a batch. Either you aren't constraining that work enough, or there is invisible work that is eating your team's capacity to execute the work in process (WIP) during a batch.

2. *Impose WIP Constraints.*[9]

Ramp meters constrain the inflow of new vehicles on the crowded freeway. During bad weather or when there is congestion at the destination, the air traffic control imposes a ground stop at the originating airport. On a busy evening, the restaurants stop taking reservations after a certain number of tables have been booked. All these are examples of work-in-process (WIP) constraints to maintain the operational flow.

Cycle time, which we are trying to shorten, can also be expressed as the amount of time the work spends as WIP. Therefore, a predictable cycle time requires constraining the WIP.

Starting with a small batch size is a big first step in doing that. But you have to go a step further. You have to make the work visible. The most widely used system for making WIP visible is the Kanban system adapted from the Toyota Production System (TPS). Representing a queue of development work on a Kanban board is simple. You show your work items as work you will start next (backlog), work currently in process (in process), and work that has been just completed (done).

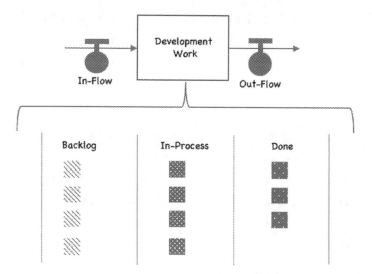

Figure 6-3. *Kanban board of the development work*

So the stock of development work in Figure 6-2 can be expanded as illustrated in Figure 6-3. When the units of work (i.e., user stories) are written clearly, everyone involved can see what's in progress with a Kanban board. Not only that, they should be able to see a working software demo of the completed work and what is queued up next to be worked upon. Instead of cycle time, the managers should get curious about how the work flows from backlog to done through managing the in-process queue.

The real art of managing WIP isn't in setting some arbitrary limits on user stories in backlog or in process queues; it is in what to do when you see them lengthening.

But before you should worry about managing WIP, you have to know all your WIP. There might be work happening that you can't even see. Usually only the planned new work is readily visible. Outside of that, there could be unplanned and unpredictable ad hoc work requests that are taking up your team's bandwidth. For my teams, these often showed up as production support requests and custom sales enablement work supporting in-flight sales deals. Invisible work can also manifest as dependencies that prevent work from happening—poor system architecture, work waiting on external dependencies, or an expert resource that everyone relies on. The work required to resolve such dependencies is the WIP you don't see.

Before you begin managing the queues, you have to know all the queues. Before you begin managing the WIP, you have to know all the WIP.

When any of the queues gets long, the simplest WIP constraint is to block new demand—stop the intake of new work into the queue. This could be a blunt approach because some new requirements may be of high business value. So to have a surplus of high-value items, you have to purge the low-value work from the queue first. This is no different from hospitals moving noncritical patients out of the ER so that more critical patients can occupy the ER beds.

But deciding WIP constraints based on relative value of work requires up-front work to translate business requirements into precise user stories such that their relative business value is clear and verifiable. Even though software project estimates are typical based on the initial business requirements, they never represent the actual work content of the project. Due to the prevalence of the Scrum methodology, the executable work is often documented as user stories. The initial business requirements need unpacking, sometimes a lot of unpacking, to understand the user problem and define the hypothesis of an appropriate solution as a high-quality user story. It can be time consuming. But it is needed. Because this process to understand the specific business value serves as a good filter to shed low-value requirements even before they get into the backlog.

Folks often use the term *backlog grooming*. That doesn't mean just writing whatever user stories you can. It actually means doing all the legwork to understand relative and specific business value of each user story. This grooming work for the next batch has to happen while the current batch is executing. Sometimes a term called *dual-track Scrum* is used to refer to this approach.

Blocking new demand and purging low-value work are examples of demand-side WIP constraints. WIP can also be managed by some supply-side approaches. As discussed earlier, when you want to deliver work on a fixed cadence, adding capacity or increasing capacity utilization isn't a good idea because it adds to the cycle time. One thing that does work from my experience is having a versatility of skill set within your development team. Senior developers should be able to help you shape business requirements into a work backlog. QA engineers should be able to help with development work, and vice versa, if the need arises. If the work involves multiple software technologies, it is prudent to have your developers cross-trained so that you resolve emerging queues with people from within the team. You are resolving supply constraints on finishing work by cultivating versatility in the work capacity, instead of adding new people from outside.

3. *Build in a Cadence.*[10]

When the trains run on a timely cadence, the passengers aren't eager to pile into just the one on the platform, because they know the next one is right around the corner. So is the case with software development cycles. If you can't deliver working software on a fixed cadence, it will be impossible for you to develop in small batches or impose constraints on WIP, because your customer won't trust you and they will try to force all requirements into the earliest possible batch.

Delivering on a frequent cadence is what makes small batches possible. But for enterprises not used to it, it can be a proverbial chicken and egg problem. Enterprise IT practitioners often gripe that while they want to deliver in small batches, their business stakeholders won't let them. I believe it is disingenuous to expect the business to trust the development team unilaterally. The development team has to buy into the small-batch approach first, and show progress on a fixed cadence through working software, to build that trust with their internal or external customers.

It is easier to ask your business to wait for one or two weeks as compared with a few months to see progress. Along with the progress, when they can provide feedback and reprioritize their requirements after each cycle in the cadence, they start having an engagement with the development process that engenders trust. Without this mutual trust between business and technical stakeholders, it is naive to expect cadence-oriented delivery with small batches and constrained WIP.

Even when there is desire to operate on trust, the best efforts to deliver on a short cadence often come undone due to reasons not controlled either by the business stakeholders or developers. It could be a tightly coupled system architecture, as described in the Complexity Principle, that makes a small change impossible without breaking things elsewhere. It could be due to lack of a dynamic software stack, as reviewed in the Stack Principle, as a result of which the developers have to fiddle with the entire stack to implement a small change. Not only that, but it could

147

even be a poor development infrastructure for your stack that makes continuous cadence of software delivery impossible for customers to provide frequent and reliable feedback.

Nicole Forsgren, Jez Humble, and Gene Kim, in their well-researched book *Accelerate*, discuss the foundations to implement continuous-cadence delivery. The key theme of those foundations is automation of repetitive work.[11] Whether it is managing configuration of software systems or integrating newly developed software into an existing system or automated testing, *maximizing the amount of work not done* through automation is a critical requirement for delivering software on a frequent cadence. Having automated development infrastructure for continuous delivery of software on a frequent cadence is the technical foundation of the business trust that enables working in small batches and applying WIP constraints.

Jeff Lawson of Twilio describes in his book *Ask Your Developer* how lack of good infrastructure nearly toppled his company when they were growing rapidly[12]:

... the build would actually fail a substantial number of times—at worst, up to 50 percent of the time—and the developer would have to start over again. We regularly lost days of productivity just getting code out. This was the opposite of moving fast.

Writing the code wasn't the hard part. Wrangling our antiquated systems was. Talk about a self-inflicted wound. As a result, our best engineers started quitting, frustrated at the inability to do their jobs. At first it was a few, and before we knew it, nearly half of our engineers had quit. Half! It was an absolute disaster, and it almost tanked the company.

The requirement for a good DevSecOps infrastructure within your stack that enables fast cadence often gets bucketed as a nonfunctional requirement. Because customers don't see the direct effect of such an infrastructure, the management questions the related investments. But when you are developing software to innovate fast, an investment in the operational infrastructure of your stack becomes a functional need because it makes the trains run on time.

4. *Exploit Beneficial Variability.*[13]

The pursuit for operational efficiency within enterprise technology groups takes a grim look at all sources of variability. That view is accurate when you are building software for *digitization* or *digitalization*. But when you are building to innovate, you have to distinguish between variability that adds value and that doesn't. Just as nature innovates through selective pressures on beneficial variations, enterprises must innovate by leveraging beneficial variability and reducing undesirable variability.

Risk taking is central to innovation. Insisting on full ROI on every software investment is a surefire path to mediocre solutions. To understand, let us compare two choices:

A: An investment of $100,000 with an expected payoff of $1,000,000 success probability of 50%

B: An investment of $100,000 with an expected payoff of $200,000 success probability of 100%

Choice B has lower uncertainty, but it isn't the best economic choice. When you desire asymmetric payoffs that are associated with choice A, you have to make decisions based on expected economic payoff. I am not arguing that you should embrace every risk, but pointing out that asymmetric expected payoffs are an example source of beneficial variability that should be exploited.

In fact, a lack of practical awareness of such asymmetric payoffs is what prevents enterprise companies from investing in things like software development infrastructure. Everyone espouses the need for constant innovation in enterprise, but I rarely see risk taking based on payoffs. There is constant exhortatory pressure for developers to deliver fast, but there is a lot of reluctance to spend on infrastructure that makes developers more productive.

Just as there could be unwillingness to exploit beneficial variabilities, there is equal unwillingness to eliminate undesirable variabilities. Take the case of forecasting errors. We have discussed the problem of sacred project plans before. The vast majority of projects miss the plan in some dimension. Yet, we try hard to conform to each one we create. Think of all the convoluted narratives spun around the status reports explaining red, yellow, and green statuses. When large projects don't pan out, they become even larger. Even more thorough planning and more people get added to the project.

That is the opposite of what the remedy should be. Instead, we need to move in the opposite direction. A shorter planning horizon represents the most significant opportunity to improve the performance of enterprise software projects. With small batches and constrained WIPs, short planning horizons enable rapid customer feedback. In the Age of Software, when enterprises have to rely on external supply chains, short plans also allow developers to keep up pace with fast-evolving cloud-based software technologies.

5. *Decentralize Decision Making.*[14]

When building for new and differentiated business value, we need to aim for dynamic control over the development process—a control that isn't merely trying to minimize deviations from a static plan, but a formal control system that discovers and maximizes business value. Because software is evolving so fast, most opportunities to maximize value from software are only encountered by the developers building the software. But they are so attuned to avoid unwanted deviations from the plan they don't take or aren't empowered to take any immediate action to exploit those opportunities.

Flow-based management centers decentralizing decision making control as much as possible such that the emphasis is on accepting deviations if they increase the business value.

To optimize flow, implementing a strategy of agility (outlined in the Culture Principle) is critical for any innovative software development exercise. A dynamic stack is the foundation of agility. An Agile culture is the source of agility. The flow management techniques help realize the value of that agility. Stack, culture, and flow are essential to leverage the real agility of software for rapid innovation, because together they help in decentralizing decision making at the level at which development happens.

As we learned from the maneuver warfare, a small, autonomous team operating at a proximity to their customer has to be the unit where all development decisions are made. These empowered teams have to be managed through two-way responsibility contracts. Teams have to be assigned meaningful problems to solve, not fixed specs to deliver. They need psychological security so that they are comfortable providing back information on possible deviations that can be opportunities to increase value.

Just as the principles of maneuver warfare are foundational to the strategy of agility, the concepts of flow are foundational to the tactics of agility. When assessing progress, working software should be the only way to assess progress against stated objectives, in a context where all ongoing work is visible to everyone. For that to happen, flow concepts of working in small batches, constraining WIP, and leveraging cadence provide the process mechanisms.

A management approach based on centralized control should only be leveraged for business problems that are infrequent and large. An enterprise replacing a home-grown ERP system with standardized SAP software would need a centralized large program approach. I had described such projects earlier as projects of *digitization* or *digitalization* variety, from the ones that require rapid customer-focused innovation. An organization with a rapidly growing customer base won't benefit from a big one-time CRM software implementation. When the goal is customer-focused innovation, a decentralized flow-based approach is the only option that works.

As I have argued earlier, as *software eats the enterprise*, the business need for software-driven innovation is rapidly increasing. Everyone is implementing the same software. The way to differentiate is innovating on what is possible with what is available. For that conundrum, enterprise companies that only commission infrequent and centralized software transformation programs will never match the pace of the ones that focus on a decentralized flow-based approach.

Managing Flow to Avoid Queues

Accruing repeatable and predictable business value through software investments is creative work. For such work, the management objective mustn't be optimizing some forecasted project timeline or budget. It mustn't just recycle methodologies superficially to shift from project to product management. Instead, it must get laser focused on discovering and exploiting the most fertile paths of development. It must move the locus of development closer to customer feedback, not to do exactly what they ask or want, but use their feedback as a source of information, as a filter to shift focus on what paths to pursue and what paths to abandon.

The business requirements never correlate directly to scope of development. They are ideas. These ideas are stocks of information that *flow* to become stocks of value when translated to working software. The process is complex since it involves a web of interconnections between developers, software system, management, and market needs. When information flow between these interconnections is continuous and decentralized, it makes the flow of business value from software development continuous. To illustrate, we can update the diagram in Figure 6-4 as in the following.

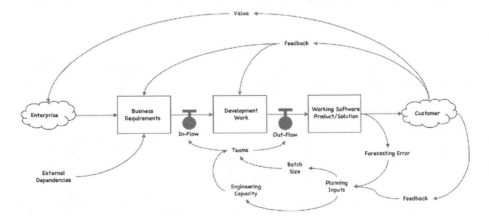

Figure 6-4. *Dynamic flows of information, software, and value*

In the absence of this continuous and decentralized flow, innovation isn't possible. Donald Reinertsen describes this decentralized information flow as[15]

> *When high-quality decentralized economic information is absent, it is too often replaced by the mind-numbing bureaucracy of centralized control.*

All the Agile techniques are based on flow management techniques for queue management. These methods are often implemented without creating the dynamic stack foundation and an Agile culture. As a result, it is the same centralized management redressed in new methods.

The concepts of flow provide the tangible process mechanisms to link the decentralized information flow to software development in ways that result in repeatable and predictable business value. These mechanisms work because they help in identifying and managing emergent long queues of work within the development. When leveraged with a dynamic stack, and in a truly Agile culture, they provide a path to unlock the agility possible with software-based innovation.

Long queues of development work must be avoided because they hinder dynamic flow of information that is so critical to making efficient interventions in a complex system that a software development for new and differentiated business value is. That frees up humans involved in software development—developers and management—to be creative and solve customer problems. It reorients software development to put faith in the human prowess to effect human progress, instead of in technology or methods.

The Flow Principle   Manage development flow, not project or product timelines.

Key Tenets:

- The real deliverable of software development work isn't a project or a product. It is to create business value that is repeatable and predictable.

- We have to stop retrofitting old ways of software management into Agile methodologies. What we actually need is to *reorient* back to managing the flow of business value through software development.

- To achieve that, the focus must shift from *delivery-based* management to *flow-based* management within enterprise software.

- Software development is a complex system of entities—people (developers, management, customers), software system, and business requirements—interconnected in ways that it is impossible to predict and control its behavior.

- You need a management framework that embraces the complexity of various information loops that come from the interconnections. That is where flow-based management approach comes in.

- Instead of managing people or business requirements or forecasts, it focuses on optimizing the information flow across the interconnections within the software development lifecycle.

- The following are the levers of flow-based management to create repeatable and predictable value from the software development cycle:

  - Reduce your batch size of development to reduce cycle time and increase the frequency of customer feedback.

  - Impose work-in-process constraints to make cycle time predictable.

  - Build and deliver in cadence to create trust for cycle times.

  - Exploit beneficial variability as a source of new information.

  - Decentralize decision making to leverage creativity of your developers and teams.

References

[1]   Reinertsen, D. G. (2009). *The Principles of Product Development Flow: Second Generation Lean Product Development* (first ed. on Kindle, page 53). Celeritas.

[2]   Reinertsen, D. G. (2009). *The Principles of Product Development Flow: Second Generation Lean Product Development* (first ed. on Kindle, page 11). Celeritas.

[3]   Reinertsen, D. G. (2009). *The Principles of Product Development Flow: Second Generation Lean Product Development* (first ed. on Kindle, page 112). Celeritas.

[4]   Agile Alliance. (2001). *Principles behind the Agile Manifesto.* Manifesto for Agile Software Development. `https://agilemanifesto.org/principles.html`

[5]   *Reinertsen, D. G. (2009). The Principles of Product Development Flow: Second Generation Lean Product Development (first ed. on Kindle, page 5). Celeritas.*

[6]   *Reinertsen, D. G. (2009). The Principles of Product Development Flow: Second Generation Lean Product Development (first ed. on Kindle, page 56). Celeritas.*

[7]   *Meadows, D. H. (2008). Thinking in Systems: A Primer (Chapter 1). Chelsea Green.*

[8]   *Reinertsen, D. G. (2009). The Principles of Product Development Flow: Second Generation Lean Product Development (first ed. on Kindle, Chapter 5). Celeritas.*

[9]   *Reinertsen, D. G. (2009). The Principles of Product Development Flow: Second Generation Lean Product Development (first ed. on Kindle, Chapter 6). Celeritas.*

[10] *Reinertsen, D. G. (2009). The Principles of Product Development Flow: Second Generation Lean Product Development (first ed. on Kindle, Chapter 7). Celeritas.*

[11] *Forsgren, N., Humble, J., & Kim, G. (2018). Accelerate: The Science Behind DevOps: Building and Scaling High Performing Technology Organizations (Chapter 9). IT Revolution Press.*

[12] *Lawson, J. (2021). Ask Your Developer: How to Harness the Power of Software Developers and Win in the 21st Century (Kindle ed., page 251) Harper Business.*

[13]   *Reinertsen, D. G. (2009). The Principles of Product Development Flow: Second Generation Lean Product Development (first ed. on Kindle, Chapter 4). Celeritas.*

[14]   *Reinertsen, D. G. (2009). The Principles of Product Development Flow: Second Generation Lean Product Development* (first ed. on Kindle, Chapter 9). Celeritas.

[15]   Reinertsen, D. G. (2009). *The Principles of Product Development Flow: Second Generation Lean Product Development* (first ed. on Kindle, page 28). Celeritas.

PART 3

Transitioning from Good to Great

Subscribing to the preceding principles will make your enterprise a good software company. To become a great software company, you have to let your people thrive.

Empower your Teams and Manage software development as a creative process. Trust your human talent to take you from good to great, as explained in the following principles.

CHAPTER 7

Teams Build Good Software, Not Resources

The Team Principle

Ways must be found to reward design managers for keeping their organizations lean and flexible. There is need for a philosophy of system design management which is not based on the assumption that adding manpower simply adds to productivity. The development of such a philosophy promises to unearth basic questions about value of resources and techniques of communication which will need to be answered before our system-building technology can proceed with confidence.

—Melvin E. Conway

The essence of the "Team Software" philosophy is that the behavior of a team maps directly to the qualities of its product, and vice versa. If you want a product with certain characteristics, you must ensure that the team has those characteristics before the product's development.

—Jim and Michele McCarthy

© Amarinder Sidhu 2023
A. Sidhu, *Becoming a Software Company*, https://doi.org/10.1007/978-1-4842-9169-6_7

What is needed is a vision rooted in human nature so noble, so attractive that it not only attracts the uncommitted and magnifies the spirit and strength of its adherents, but also undermines the dedication and determination of any competitors or adversaries. Moreover, such a unifying notion should be so compelling that it acts as a catalyst or beacon around which to evolve those qualities that permit a collective entity or organic whole to improve its stature in the scheme of things.

—John Boyd

I have developed a strong dislike for an often repeated question: *How many resources do you need to deliver this <project, product, feature, capability>?*

The version of me from 12 years ago would at least make a sincere attempt to respond, even though the question caused me some discomfort. If you have ever done software coding in your life, you know that resource estimates never pan out. But I tried to make as informed a guess as possible, because that's what you were supposed to do when you were asked.

Not anymore. Now, if the request is aligned with the mission of a current team, the request goes on the backlog after a proper vetting of the need. For a new project or product initiative, my response is simply: *we need to build a team, first.*

I have realized that the source of my instant discomfort or dislike toward the question was the implicit assertion that people are "resources." They are not. But even if you can look past the implications of using the term "resources" for humans, there is a larger issue.

Planning work by allocating people as "resources" hinders the realization of the true potential of the software revolution. It is an anti-pattern. In software development, anti-patterns are common practices that yield undesirable results. Of those undesirable results, cost overruns and timeline delays are the visible ones. But mediocre software is the result that isn't.

The "resources" anti-pattern abstracts unique individuals into a soulless category. It creates and furthers a perverse delusion that human beings can be modeled as quantities, which can be estimated, budgeted, and allocated. This delusion is the legacy of the industrial age. Back then, after the management secured raw materials, equipment, and machines, human workers were the "resource" to be flexed to scale production of template goods. It worked then because the management problem was to replicate and scale the production of the template goods, even though at a human cost. The same approach worked within enterprise IT when there was new value in just implementing the latest commercial enterprise software packages at the lowest cost possible.

Not anymore. Software ate the enterprise, and creating new value requires innovating on the use cases. You can stay ahead of the latest digital transformation trends as much as you can. You can be as diligent as you can be in following the social proof of your industry peers for leveraging technology. But if you do what everyone else is doing, you will only get market average return on software investments. To create new value with new use cases, similar to how active investment managers competing with market indexed funds look for alpha, you have to look for alpha.[1]

What is a source of alpha in the context of enterprise software? It is not the customer. As we discussed in the Value Principle, the customers only know what they want when they see it. The real source of innovation, the alpha, is a team operating in a culture that allows it to be creative[2] and to achieve its most optimal flow.[3] It is a team that is allowed to build the right solution for the customer's progress.

---

[1] Alpha is the excess return over the market indexed return. www.investopedia.com/terms/a/alpha.asp

[2] The Culture Principle, Chapter 5.

[3] The Flow Principle, Chapter 6.

In the Age of Software, the raw material is the ideas possessed by the individuals within a team. The recipe of converting those ideas into repeatable and predictable business value is often unknown in advance. Therefore, the management problem is not scaling the production of a template good. It is to scale putting the new ideas into software-based production.

We know that software once produced can be copied infinitely. The marginal cost of each new unit of software product is close to zero. But before you achieve a high-value production scenario like that, you have to make a certain number of attempts at discovering value. And each value attempt has to be an effort, in part or in whole, to fulfill an unmet customer need.[1] Whether you will need a few or many attempts can't be determined in advance. It is impossible to create a project plan for it.

Therefore, you must entrust a team to navigate this essential complexity of creating value with software.[4] The value never correlates to your managerial prowess at resource allocation. In a world where the primary goal is creating new business value through new intellectual property, resources can be allocated wisely only by an "infinitely wise centralized decision maker," as Donald Reinertsen reminds us[2]:

> *Resource is allocated by an infinitely wise centralized decision maker. There is no explicit cost for requesting priority or excess resource. In theory, the decision maker has the scarce global knowledge needed to allocate resources. In reality, this creates a massive incentive for projects to exaggerate their needs. Skillful lobbying can often get more resources than legitimate needs.*

I have never come across such decision makers.

---

[4] The Complexity Principle, Chapter 3.

If "resources" is an anti-pattern, "team" is the pattern antidote. Teams build good and valuable software, not some arbitrary collection of resources. A team is the fundamental unit of software engineering. This has to be understood and practiced as a management ideal. In the Age of Software, the primary management deliverable is not on time and within budget delivery. It is to build teams and create organizational environments those teams can thrive in.

"Team = Software": Team as a Management Deliverable

Team shouldn't be considered as just a concept that applies to the software developers, that is, people that build the actual software. We can extend it and assign it to all levels as we traverse through the corporate ranks.

Let's call the team that delivers the actual software as a level 1 team. The managers of this team are a level 2 team. Level 2's deliverable is building the level 1 team. Any discrepancy in level 1 is a reflection on level 2's teamwork, not just level 1's fault. This pattern applies to all levels that might exist above levels 1 and 2 in the corporate hierarchy.[5]

Jim and Michele McCarthy defined this framework of thinking about a team as a management deliverable.[3] They called it the "Team = Software" philosophy. It is a powerful idea because it creates a strong incentive for accountability at all levels. Throwing the level 1 team under the bus for a poor outcome on a software initiative doesn't work anymore. The failure of level 1 is on level 2 and so on and so forth.

---

[5] Hopefully not too many levels though, because a long hierarchy reduces the bandwidth for the fast information flow required for rapid value creation.

While it is useful for every type of organization to adopt this thinking, "Team = Software" was defined keeping in mind the context of software companies or organizations trying to *become* software companies. It was defined for organizations trying to build new intellectual property (IP) with software.

Therefore, it follows from the "Team = Software" philosophy that creating a team is the first and foremost deliverable—not the actual product or solution. Any group of developers has to build mutual trust and mutual experience before it starts performing at its full creative potential. It is the management's responsibility (immediate levels above) to shepherd them through an initial ramp-up phase. This is the managerial work that is often glossed over in the enterprise software planning and execution.

How long does it take a particular team to come together? The answer to this question depends on the people in the team and how long it takes to get them to a settled and trusted place. A manager who wants a high-performing team or teams should spend the majority of their time on building and developing their teams. A well-understood part of that is recruiting and hiring. Something not as well understood is that the managers have to model the behaviors and virtues that they want to see in their teams. That is what the "Team = Software" philosophy insists.

It isn't too different from parenting. It isn't about what you say; it is about what you do. If you want your kid not to yell at you, you have to stop yelling at them. Similarly, the teams take after the behavior modeled by their managers. If you want the team to be transparent on where it stands, you as a manager have to be transparent about your objectives and expectations.

This philosophy is the reason for my insistence on building a team in response to the resources question. I really like the philosophy because it creates the right stake for everyone in the software product being built, in the new IP being built. While only frontline developers may be building the actual software, managers have to work on getting the structure of the team's communication and empowerment right. The managers have to set up the right development infrastructure that allows for optimal development flow.[6] Perhaps the most critical of all software management aspects, an enterprise has to look at the agility of the business decision making with the lens of achieving the desired software development agility.

From a top-down perspective, if you prioritize building software cheaply, you will get the *cheap* software. If you prioritize that your teams meet the timeline forecasts, you will get *on-time* software. Whether any of that software creates the intended business value, that requires an entirely different incentive. Everyone from top to bottom has to model the behaviors and virtues that emphasize creating value. The "Team = Software" philosophy provides a framework to align the incentives aligned for everyone in the software organization. In the words of the McCarthys, it makes it so that everyone is accountable for the same thing:

> *Even though we were bosses, we could not fault a team for lacking a virtue, unless and until we had personally demonstrated it. Nor could we expect any remedy that we weren't personally modeling.*

What Do You Want to Ship? Is That in Your Org Chart?

Once you form an organization with a small team–oriented structure, you have to pay attention to the communication patterns between those teams. This follows from an observation about organizational design made by computer scientist Melvin Conway in a 1968 research paper. Conway wrote[4]:

---

[6] The Flow Principle, Chapter 6.

> *Organizations which design systems are constrained*
> *to produce systems which are copies of the*
> *communication structures of these organizations.*

Initially, a seemingly innocuous conclusion of a paper in an IT journal, the observation was later dubbed as *Conway's Law* by Fred Brooks in a highly popular 1985 book in the software circles, *The Mythical Man-Month.*[5] Since then, Conway's Law has stood the test of time and isn't something that should be taken lightly.

At its core, Conway's observation implies that the architecture of the software system will be similar to the structure of the organization that built it.[6] Whatever you want to ship with your software system or service has to be modeled in the structure of the development organization.

Take a typical example of an enterprise software project, when an enterprise company outsources the system development to a systems integrator consulting firm. In such a scenario, there are three teams at a minimum: one from the enterprise company's staff involved in the project, another an onsite team of consultants, and another an offshore team of consultants.

If you apply Conway's Law here, this system should have at least three subsystems built separately by these teams. Depending on how big the system is, and subscribing to the Two-Pizza Rule for each team, there may be a need for more subsystems that will need to interface with each other. This type of structure is required because the communication will be the deepest and most informal within a team as compared with across teams. If you want to avoid productivity being killed by endless meetings across teams, you have to limit the interactions among the teams, necessarily so. Instead of a plethora of meetings, these teams have to engage through specific and published interfaces, such as "how to work with us" written documents or APIs, broadly available to other teams.

You can keep expecting a flexible system with a modular design, but you aren't going to get it if you build a large team that has a single centralized control. You have to plan for the modularity you need and vest the control to the specific team building it. Therein, the management shouldn't merely focus on directing the teams. Instead, it should focus on how the various teams communicate with each other—as specifications based and structured as possible.

Fowler goes on to suggest, "Accepting Conway's Law is superior to ignoring it." That seems to be more or less happening in successful product software companies. The microservices architecture pattern, quite prevalent in web-based systems today, is a practical outcome of and is an acceptance of Conway's Law. Read how Jeff Lawson describes that coming about at Amazon[7]:

> As Amazon split the organization up into small teams, they also kept carving up the code into small pieces so the teams could "take it with them" and operate it independently. These teams and their respective code needed a way to talk to each other, and "web services" turned out to be the answer. Instead of each team shipping code into some giant repository that somebody else would deploy and run on servers, each team would run their own code as a service that other teams could interoperate with. Because each team was small, the surface area of their service was typically somewhat limited as well. Over time, these became known as "microservices" because each individual service typically did one thing, and did it well.

The API of each team's microservice is the structured communication mechanism to follow for outside teams that need to communicate with that team.

Take another example of how Conway's Law can play out in an organization vis-à-vis the communication from the management to the executing teams. Consider the following question as a management team: Are you assigning business problems to your teams and empowering them to solve them the right way? Or are you asking them to do specific things by a certain date?

You will get vastly different outcomes with these two approaches. There is a higher probability of an innovative solution with the former as compared with the latter. This is because an organization's governance mechanism, its approach to problem solving, and communication patterns constrain the solution space.[8] The first question emphasizes creativity and building the right thing. The second incentivizes the team to prioritize meeting a deadline and just focus on shipping on time.

That is why just adopting the tactic of building a product team instead of a project team doesn't work in enterprise companies. If the teams are operating within an organization structure that expects compliance to the provided specifications and specified timelines, your product team will merely operate as a feature team, no different from what happens to it as a project team.

In addition to these, there is another insight from Conway's paper that is perhaps the most important to internalize as far as the theme of this book is concerned:

> *Because the design that occurs first is almost never*
> *the best possible, the prevailing system concept may*
> *need to change. Therefore, flexibility of organization*
> *is important to effective design.*

A new and innovative system design requires many iterations or will undergo many changes. That requires a flexible organizational structure that is amenable to changes. A development organization consisting of small autonomous teams, interfacing with each other through structured interfaces (technical or otherwise), is the only structure that fits the bill for that need, because swapping a small team (with their subsystem or a module) is easier than a broader reorganization.

Aligning With, Within, and Across Teams: The Need for a Writing Culture as a Good Software Practice

While we are on the topic of communication patterns, the one pattern that deserves specific attention is how teams share information with each other—the ubiquitous use of PowerPoint as a communication device. The use of *slideware* to summarize information and present decision options is rampant across various levels of enterprise software. Developers use it to communicate among themselves and embed it in their Jira user stories. Managers use it to communicate upward and sideways. Executives use it to make and communicate decisions downward and sideways.

Outside maybe a few enlightened organizations, it isn't a stretch to say that *slideware is most of the organizational thoughtware.* And since thoughtware is the starting point of most software systems, it is worth examining if this reliance on slideware is a good practice as a communication pattern.

Several years ago, I attended a day-long session in Boston's Seaport Hotel on analyzing and presenting information from Edward Tufte, a master information designer from Yale University. Mid-presentation, Tufte launched into a compelling critique of using PowerPoint as a communication device. I was so persuaded by Tufte's argument that I ended up buying his book on the topic.

Edward Tufte writes the following in his book *The Cognitive Style of PowerPoint*[9]: "PowerPoint is presenter-oriented, not content-oriented, not audience-oriented." A great presenter can lead a group to a bad decision. A poor PowerPoint-driven presentation can lead to confusion and eliminate good ideas from consideration. A boring presentation makes a group indifferent to what is being presented. So much of the information delivery utilizing PowerPoint depends on the efficacy of the presentation.

But does that have to be so for developing software?

Tufte presents an alternative: when we are looking to align people across the organization, we should instead look for an alternative that is "content-oriented" and "audience-oriented." Tufte goes on to argue, "As analysis becomes more causal, multivariate, comparative, evidence-based, and resolution-intense, the more damaging the bullet list becomes."

Building software of creative value, building new software IP is exactly that—a complex exercise of involving many details and variables and requiring customer evidence. Tufte's recommendation for an alternate to cover gaps on PowerPoint is very straightforward:

> *For serious presentations, replace PP with word-processing or page-layout software. Making this transition in large organizations requires a straightforward executive order: From now on your presentation software is Microsoft Word, not PowerPoint. Get used to it.*

That's what Amazon has done very successfully—replace PowerPoint with narrative writing in Word. Bezos followed Tufte's recommendation, quite literally, because the narrative structure of Word requires deeper thought and better understanding of causal relations between information.[10] It has been so successful at Amazon that they have published a full methodology called "Working Backwards" (WB) that relies on narrative writing. We use a variation of WB within my teams as a starting point for any new initiative of software development.

Whether you use WB as a methodology is an organizational choice. But it is clear that narrative-style writing is a better and more credible alternative for information exchange for alignment with, within, and across teams. It is what other successful software organizations like Stripe have also done.

Stripe's writing culture is regarded as a differentiator for the company.[11] CEO's emails are known to have footnotes. Writing is what makes their team-oriented organization effective. Their emphasis on teams is unique in the sense that they are open to acquiring whole teams. At Stripe, you can apply to join the company as a team.[12]

Jim and Michele McCarthy describe in their book that the primary issue for failure of a collaborative effort for creating new intellectual property is never the "headcount shortage." It is the inability to "make the heads you have count."[13] Writing by driving better alignment aids in making heads count.

Writing is also something that can make a team-oriented organization effective in a remote context, because it is not the "physical distance" that becomes a problem in remote work. It is the "psychological distance."[14] Narrative writing, when done right, can close that gap.

Writing can also help avoid the problems associated with forcing a verbal consensus within groups. Ask ten people to get an ice cream, but with a complete consensus, they'll pick chocolate or vanilla every time.[7] Groups of people will never agree on what's innovative or interesting. They tend to agree on paths of least resistance or sway toward a loud voice with power. Such a *consensus* only paves the way toward mediocrity. If the same people have to consider and provide written feedback for their choice of flavor, more interesting options will emerge.

Narrative writing that describes the business problem and potential solutions is a proven tool for increasing the engagement ("making the heads count") and a forcing mechanism for achieving alignment. It helps align people with, within, and across teams at all levels by increasing the information resolution (causal and multivariate analysis with evidence) and by boosting the bandwidth of communications. Whether it is an

---

[7] The Vanilla Ice Cream Principle. I read this in a newsletter from Write of Passage (https://writeofpassage.school).

executive communicating strategy or a level 1 team member writing user stories, cultivating the practice of good narrative writing can go a long way in increasing the value of intellectual property embedded within software.

The Challenge of Communicating "Higher Purpose"

While a team collective is made up of individuals, just having individuals doesn't guarantee a team collective. A team coalesces around individuals who operate within a culture of agility, around individuals who aren't micromanaged. A team solidifies around individuals who have built *mutual trust*, around individuals who operate on *intuitive knowledge*. We learned this from Chet Richard's application of maneuver warfare principles to business environments that mutual trust and intuitive knowledge are foundational to a good team. But the team transitions from good to great when the individuals involved share creative motivation.

Companies use "vision statements" or "mission statements" to describe frameworks of creative motivation. But many such visions and missions are "lifeless" or "lame."[15] Employees don't believe in them. Customers don't understand them, because they are created as mandatory items for driving PR or underline corporate marketing communications. As a result, the required effect of these statements percolating into the decision making of level 1 teams creating software never comes to a pass. If that wasn't the case, everyone with a team of software developers at their disposal would be creating new intellectual property all the time.

How to write good vision and mission statements is out of scope for this book. I am actually interested in a very specific question: how to define a *higher purpose* for the development teams.

To come up with a potential answer, I will revisit two concepts we encountered earlier in the book: (1) communicating missions as responsibility contracts for teams and (2) leveraging business strategy as a focusing device.[8]

Let us look at an example from professional sports to understand. The NBA player Shane Battier was described by famed author Michael Lewis as "a replaceable cog" in a basketball league "driven by superstars." But Battier somehow increased the winning ability of every team he played on. For that reason, Lewis called him the "No-Stats All-Star."[16]

Shane also knows a lot about team dynamics. He describes four types of teams based on where they rank on mutual trust and mission focus—*disastrous*, *lagging*, *brittle*, and *gel*. [17] A *disastrous* team, as the name suggests, can be easily observed and intervened on quickly. On the other end of the spectrum, there are *gel* teams that win championships. A *gel* team doesn't have a high-frequency occurrence; you know it when you see it. In most instances then, the prevalent archetype for a team is either *lagging* or *brittle*. The million- or billion-dollar question then becomes: what is the ingredient to transition from lagging or brittle to a *gel* team?

Those ingredients are cultivating trust and building a long term focus towards a mission (Figure 7-1).

---

[8] Mission and focus are two other aspects of the Boydian concept of maneuver warfare, in addition to mutual trust and intuitive knowledge (the Culture Principle, Chapter 5).

Figure 7-1. *Shane Battier's four types of teams*

In professional sports, the mission is straightforward: win a championship. In a business environment, however, there are no discrete trophies to win every season, certainly not at the level 1 or 2 teams building software. That is why the concept of communicating missions to those teams clearly becomes very critical.

The mission has to be specific and devoted to a single purpose. Even if there are no trophies to win, the mission has to describe what "winning" looks like for a team. The framing of the "winning" context is important because people want to be on winning teams. The trust within the team improves when they navigate the highs and lows while trying to win. And nothing cures the motivational malaise more than doing work that leads to a market win or a marketplace success.

The mission, therefore, is what makes the team gel. The mission doesn't have to be something grandiose, but it has to be definitely clear. For example, the various checks performed—safety checks, compliance, etc.—when a driver goes online are owned by different teams at Uber. The "winning" for each of these teams is solving problems that delay those checks so that driver onboarding is fast.

In addition to this type of clarity, it is critical for the team to understand and to own the responsibility of finding and building the actual solution for business problems that are aligned to the mission. For that, the team should have a deep understanding of the customer's *needs*. It needs to have a strong *belief* that it can build the right solution to fulfill the need, without being micromanaged. It should perceive fulfilling the need as an *opportunity* for everyone on the team to advance their careers. The team should share the *anticipation* of a better future for their internal and external customers.[18]

The creative attractors—*need, belief, opportunity*, and *anticipation*—have to exist for the work to have a "winning" context. This is the deeper nuance for a mission to become an actual agreement—a responsibility contract that is a requirement for Agile culture.

This type of mission communication is hard within enterprise software because of the amount of work that happens from negotiated specifications. However precise the negotiation may be, the business environment changes; market needs change; technologies and development strategies change; personnel changes. This has certainly started happening in the XaaS era of enterprise software a lot more. When these changes invariably happen, the developers and teams in enterprise software, instead of suggesting creative alternatives, revert to their individual modes of survival. Because the risk of missing the specifications is so salient for them, they lie low and follow the orders until the project is completed—as per the agreed specification.

The second aspect of communicating *higher purpose* is how teams can contribute to the enterprise organization winning in the marketplace. For that, the missions have to be rooted in the organization's strategy to *win* in the marketplace. The development should not start from some "strategic plan" that is merely a description of how to get resources and manage costs of the initiative. It should start from a winning strategy of how to win, as Chet Richards argues in his book *Certain to Win*[19]:

> *At the dawn of the 21st century, strategy seems to have gone out of fashion. At the big consulting companies, strategy business is down, while billings for information systems surge. It is as if corporate leaders believe that it is more important to install technology than to understand what to do with it. This is a dangerous attitude since it is possible to spend billions implementing technology that will make the company less competitive.*

What Richards is pointing at is precisely what we learned from the cases of IBM Watson and GE Digital earlier. A highly capable technology will only create value when paired with a business strategy that is clear and actionable. If people on a team don't understand how their team's mission relates to how the whole enterprise wins, it is unlikely to fuel any creative motivation.

Therefore, the core management challenge to fuel software innovation is not managing budgets or project timelines. These things have some value, but the real challenge is in communicating *higher purpose* to the teams so that they can *gel* around it. For that, the management has to focus on creating clear missions aligned with a winning strategy and communicate them as responsibility contracts.[9]

---

[9] OKRs (Objectives and Key Results) developed by Andy Grove at Intel and popularized by John Doerr are a measurable management tool to focus and align teams around missions and strategy.

The Real Value of a Team (That Is Gelling)

I have been in and around software development for 18 years. From my experience working on teams and observing teams, when a team is gelling, it has an extra layer of emergent creativity that an equivalent collection of individuals doesn't have.

The dynamic almost has a "you know it when you see it" vibe. It is hard to manufacture this vibe into existence. It is a vibe that stems from the right organizational culture. Teams gel in an organization that has adopted the "Team = Software" philosophy and models the right behaviors at every level of hierarchy, that subscribes to the power of Conway's Law and gets its communication patterns right, and that communicates a clear higher purpose to focus the development work, instead of just shoving specifications down.

It isn't just any team, but the gelling team that makes software development "the labor that creates capital."[20] Small teams that are gelling can create outsized value. WhatsApp had 55 employees when bought by Facebook for $19 billion. Instagram had 13 employees when they were bought by Facebook for $1 billion. Within Facebook, Instagram is valued at $100 billion, but still has only about 700 employees.[21] These are relatively well-known cases, well maybe even outliers.

Let us look at some other examples. Slack had about 2500 employees when it was bought by Salesforce for $27 billion. DocuSign had grown to a $14-billion value with only 2,200 employees in 2020. Stripe, an Internet payments API company, is valued at $63 billion and has only about 7,000 employees.[22],[23] Another example of the wild west of the Internet: StreamYard, a live streaming and recording studio in a web browser, was bought by Hopin for $250 million and had just 19 employees.[24]

The point of sharing all these examples is not to highlight just the crazy valuations. It is to emphasize that when it comes to creating new intellectual property with software, the headcount doesn't matter as much. What matters is "making the heads you have count." The way to achieve that is by building teams that have a mission-oriented focus, because that is the common theme across all these examples. All of these companies have clear missions—nothing grand, just a higher purpose tied to customer progress, which is obvious to people within and outside those companies.

A gel team really is a whole more than the sum of individuals. But we must acknowledge that the phenomenon of a purely mission-driven team with a high trust quotient, which creates value like the examples just shared, is rare. Most teams, in most environments, are *directed* to build things together.[25] And in most such situations, the resulting equilibrium is acceptable to the individuals with the team and the management. To change, therefore, the onus to expect more has to be both on the individuals within teams and the management.

Every team when it has just come together will need direction. The real question that arises is whether that direction you are providing will get the team to a trusted place so that it can start operating with a mission-driven orientation or if the level of direction will just further the micromanaging equilibrium of mediocrity.

The challenge is never to micromanage a WhatsApp- or an Instagram-style homerun innovation into existence. It doesn't work that way. The challenge is to improve the organizational environment for teams to do creative work so that you can maximize the probability of a homerun innovation. That is the true purpose of a "how to win" business strategy, as well as communication of that strategy as clear missions for your teams.

Not only are gel team situations difficult to build; they can be transitory and fragile, because teams are formed from human beings and humans don't stay the same forever. Shane Battier refers to the NBA's 2010–2014 Miami Heat as a gel team. LeBron James left that team to go back to the Cleveland Cavaliers at the end of the 2014 season. And even though the Miami Heat are known for their championship culture and they are often competitive, they haven't won the championship since then.

The high trust and mission focus don't guarantee winning. And they can get compromised even in winning situations. The leadership of WhatsApp and Instagram left Facebook over disagreements on mission orientation.[26],[27] One would imagine Mark Zuckerberg, having built Facebook into a juggernaut from a plucky startup, knew a thing or two about the power of a good team.

My discussion of the gel team concept is not to admire some idealistic and unachievable notion of a team. It is to advocate that teams do their best work when allowed to operate with freedom and when equipped with a higher purpose and that the primary role of a manager at every level, and in every domain, is to communicate that purpose as clearly as possible and every day.

Embracing the Ideal of Team Building in Enterprise Software

My fundamental objective is to promote a software management ideal of a team as a unit of software engineering. The "Team = Software" philosophy and Conway's Law provide frameworks for modeling behaviors and communications for implementing the ideal. The writing culture and communication of higher purpose are mechanisms for continuously improving at the practice of this ideal.

While there is no doubt that the team-building ideal is critical to increase innovation, there is a slight wrinkle associated with applying it in enterprise software. The organizational environment is significantly different from one of a software startup. The risk profile of executing on software projects is different. You can't bet the farm and swing for the fences. Therefore, you have to be a lot more measured in applying this ideal.

That is why I want to reiterate that it has to be approached as a continuous improvement exercise. Related to that, I want to offer a few practical ideas from my personal experience of building enterprise software products within a large consulting firm.

Insource Teams. Don't Outsource Work.

If I have been able to convince you about the team being the unit of engineering, you would agree that any software systems initiative should start by acquiring the team, not negotiation of a specification. Depending on the size of the system, and because each team has to stay small, you should plan on acquiring teams proportionally to the subsystems you are building. The most critical work (corresponding to the differentiating part of your stack[10]) should reside with in-house teams. Only then you should look to insource external teams. Only once the team responsible is onboarded you should start planning the work at the subsystem level.

Plan for the Gel Time.

No team will gel from day 1. Gelling requires patience and perseverance that respects the "Team = Software" philosophy and subscribes to Conway's Law. And it is not just passive patience. It takes active diligence and requires close attention to the overall organizational structure for the initiative. Furthermore, it requires a deep understanding of every individual on the team. It requires implementing the creative attractors for the team—need, belief, opportunity, and anticipation—to build the framework of creative motivation unique to a team. It is hard work because intangibles like that don't show in the "stats column" very well (no wonder Michael Lewis called Shane Battier the No-Stats All-Star). That is why gelling doesn't happen in a culture that rewards "looking good" over "doing the right thing." The hard work to make the team gel only shows up in the outcomes of the collective team.

Obsess over Clarity of Responsibility Contracts, Not the Thoroughness of Negotiated Specifications.

The procurement process for enterprise software programs can take several months, even if you exclude the lengthy legal contract negotiations

---

[10] The Stack Principle, Chapter 4.

that follow.[11] All of that is necessitated by the inherent risk of structuring outsourced work. But what if you just insource teams? Sure, you will still need legal contracts, but at least you don't need to obsess over the thoroughness of the negotiated specifications. The time gained back can be devoted back to writing clear responsibility contracts, that is, mission statements, for each team you are insourcing. In the Age of Software, a trusted team with a mission orientation has an order of magnitude higher shelf life than a negotiated specification. There will be invariable turnover of individuals within a team. But as long as the mission has a valid business value, you can persist with a team and the intuitive knowledge that it will build.

Optimize the Delivery Flow, Not Delivery Timelines.

Once the teams are operational, and entrusted with responsibility, it is critical to build a communication process that prioritizes the flow of information. Rather than processes to communicate status, it is critical to build processes to optimize the flow of value. That means asking your teams to work in small batches and deliver working software at a frequent cadence, reviewing progress with an intent to uncover the most fertile paths to fulfill the mission,[20] not to assess whether the timelines are slipping. When the team is shipping frequently, the risk of shipping on time ebbs anyway. As a result, everyone involved can focus on shipping the right thing.

The team-building ideal, that is, the team is the fundamental unit of engineering, represents a mindset shift toward creative management from industrial management. Instead of managing resources, you shift to managing the frameworks of creative motivation for your teams. It is mandatory for the business imperative of the XaaS era of enterprise software: transitioning from implementing commercial software to innovating on possible use cases.

That's why I always insist on teams, never resources. I am imploring you to join me.

---

[11] This is why the Agile Manifesto emphasizes "customer collaboration over contract negotiation" as a core value.

The Team Principle   Build teams. Don't just hire resources, because teams build good software, not a collection of resources.

Key Tenets:

- Planning software development work by allocating people as "resources" hinders the realization of the true potential of the software revolution. It is an anti-pattern.

- This anti-pattern worked when there was new value in just implementing the latest commercial enterprise software packages at the lowest cost possible. It doesn't when enterprises have to innovate on new use cases in the Age of Software.

- The real source of innovation is a team operating in a culture that allows it to be creative and to achieve its most optimal flow. A team is the pattern antidote to the resources anti-pattern.

- Just as software is a team's deliverable, a team is management's deliverable. The managers have to model the behaviors and virtues that they want to see in their teams. This is called the "Team=Software" philosophy and can be extended to all levels of corporate hierarchy.

- The architecture of the software system will be similar to the structure of the organization that built it (Conway's Law). You can only ship what is in your org chart. To build flexible and modular systems, you have to build a small team–oriented organizational structure.

- The primary issue for failure of a collaborative effort for creating new intellectual property is never the "headcount shortage." It is the inability to "make the heads you have count."

- A good writing culture as demonstrated by organizations like Amazon and Stripe is a must for driving alignment with, within, and across teams. It reduces the psychological distance among teams.

- The core management challenge to fuel software innovation is not managing budgets or project timelines. It is in communicating *higher purpose* to the teams so that they can *gel* around it, because a gelling team can create outsized value that has no correlation with its size.

- Here's how enterprise companies can champion a good team-building ideal within their organizations:

  - Don't outsource work. Insource teams instead.

  - Always plan for gel time for new teams to build trust and create mission orientation.

  - Obsess over clarity of team responsibility contracts, not the thoroughness of negotiated specifications.

  - Always optimize the delivery flow, not delivery timelines.

References

[1]   *What Is a Value Attempt?* (2020, September 8). iiSM.org. Retrieved February 23, 2023, from https://iism.org/post/glossary-value-attempt-74

[2]   Reinertsen, D. G. (2009). *The Principles of Product Development Flow: Second Generation Lean Product Development* (Kindle ed., page 43). Celeritas.

[3]   McCarthy, J., & McCarthy, M. (2002). *Software for Your Head: Core Protocols for Creating and Maintaining Shared Vision*. Addison-Wesley.

[4]   Conway, M. E. (April 1968). *How Do Committees Invent?* Mel Conway's Homa Page. Retrieved April 14, 2023, from `www.melconway.com/Home/pdf/committees.pdf`

[5]   Brooks, F. P. (1995). *Mythical Man-Month, The: Essays on Software Engineering, Anniversary Edition* (anniversary ed., page 111). Addison-Wesley.

[6]   Fowler, M. (2022, October 20). *Conway's Law*. Martin Fowler. Retrieved April 14, 2023, from `https://martinfowler.com/bliki/ConwaysLaw.html`

[7]   Lawson, J. (2021). *Ask Your Developer: How to Harness the Power of Software Developers and Win in the 21st Century* (Kindle ed., page 37). Harper Business.

[8]   *Exploring the Duality between Product and Organizational Architectures: A Test of the "Mirroring" Hypothesis*. (2011). Harvard Business School. Retrieved April 14, 2023, from `www.hbs.edu/ris/Publication%20Files/08-039_1861e507-1dc1-4602-85b8-90d71559d85b.pdf?`

[9]   Tufte, E. R. (2006). *The Cognitive Style of PowerPoint: Pitching Out Corrupts Within* (ebook ed.). Graphics Press.

[10] Bryar, C., & Carr, B. (2021). *Working Backwards: Insights, Stories, and Secrets from Inside Amazon* (Kindle ed., page 80). St. Martin's Press.

[11] Nunez, D., & Young, S. (2020, September 2). *How Stripe Built a Writing Culture—Knock Down Silos by Slab*. Slab. Retrieved April 14, 2023, from `https://slab.com/blog/stripe-writing-culture/`

[12]   Bryant, A. (2016, April 25). *BYOT*. Stripe. Retrieved
       April 14, 2023, from `https://stripe.com/blog/bring-`
       `your-own-team`

[13]   McCarthy, J., & McCarthy, M. (2002). *Software for Your Head:
       Core Protocols for Creating and Maintaining Shared Vision*
       (page 203). Addison-Wesley.

[14]   McCarthy, J., & McCarthy, M. (2002). *Software for Your Head:
       Core Protocols for Creating and Maintaining Shared Vision*
       (page 11). Addison-Wesley.

[15]   McCarthy, J., & McCarthy, M. (2002). *Software for Your Head:
       Core Protocols for Creating and Maintaining Shared Vision*
       (page 280). Addison-Wesley.

[16]   Lewis, M. (2009, February 13). *The No-Stats All-Star*. The
       New York Times. Retrieved April 14, 2023, from `www.nytimes.`
       `com/2009/02/15/magazine/15Battier-t.html`

[17]   Battier, S., & Gupta, R. (2022, November 21). *Shane
       Battier—The No-Stats All-Star* [podcast]. Colossus, LLC. `www.`
       `joincolossus.com/episodes/68722518/battier-how-to-`
       `win?tab=transcript`

[18]   Bond, G. (2020, June 17). *Why are CEOs failing software
       engineers*. iiSM.org. Retrieved September 15, 2020, from
       `https://iism.org/article/why-are-ceos-failing-`
       `software-engineers-56`

[19]   Richards, C. (2004). *Certain to Win: The Strategy of John Boyd,
       Applied to Business* (Kindle ed., page 49). Xlibris.

[20]   Rao, V. (2018, February 8). *Rough Consensus and Maximal
       Interestingness*. Breaking Smart. `https://breakingsmart.`
       `com/en/season-1/rough-consensus-and-maximal-`
       `interestingness/`

[21]   *Billion-dollar companies with hardly any staff.* (2020, February 7). Love Money. www.lovemoney.com/ galleries/92724/billiondollar-companies-with-hardly- any-staff?page=17

[22]   Mascarenhas, N. (2023, January 12). *Stripe's internal valuation gets cut to $63 billion.* TechCrunch. Retrieved January 15, 2023, from https://techcrunch.com/2023/01/11/stripe- internal-valuation-63-billion-409a/

[23]   Kauflin, J. (2022, November 3). *Stripe Lays Off More Than 1,000 Workers, 14% Of Staff.* Forbes. Retrieved April 14, 2023, from www.forbes.com/sites/jeffkauflin/2022/11/03/ stripe-lays-off-more-than-1000-workers-14-of- staff/?sh=2589a176c1dd

[24]   Barry, N. (2022, January 22). *Tweet Thread from Nathan Barry.* https://twitter.com/nathanbarry. Retrieved April 14, 2023, from https://twitter.com/nathanbarry/statu s/1484919251219533825?s=20&t=BGm9vwOQSl2h1Dhqq6CtMw

[25]   McCarthy, J., & McCarthy, M. (2002). *Software for Your Head: Core Protocols for Creating and Maintaining Shared Vision* (page 271). Addison-Wesley.

[26]   Solon, O. (2018, April 30). *WhatsApp CEO Jan Koum quits over privacy disagreements with Facebook.* The Guardian. Retrieved April 14, 2023, from www.theguardian.com/ technology/2018/apr/30/jan-koum-whatsapp-co-founder- quits-facebook

[27]   Newton, C., & Krales, A. H. (2019, April 17). *We finally know why the Instagram founders really quit.* The Verge. Retrieved April 14, 2023, from www.theverge.com/ interface/2019/4/17/18411363/why-instagram-founders- quit-hamburger-button-location-tracking

CHAPTER 8

Practice the Art of Creative Management

The Management Principle

This is business by people who have studied to learn the art of working together. It is business by people who share a code of honor that binds them in mutual trust. It is business whose purpose is as much to know its market—the attitudes and desires of the people who might buy its product or its service— as it is to provide that product or service with integrity. It is business by people who have formed an effective team that can act and that will act swiftly and decisively to seize an opportunity, even when the opportunity arises unexpectedly. The team is not set in its ways, except in its way of doing business, which is trust of one another within the company, integrity of its product and service, appreciation of the market and potential market, and the ability to act quickly. The tempo with which the team acts, adjusts, corrects, seeks opportunity, and acts upon it, is greater than the speed of which its competitors are capable. It is greater and more powerful than the market can resist, and in that way, it wins its customers.

—*Colonel Mike Wyly*

© Amarinder Sidhu 2023
A. Sidhu, *Becoming a Software Company*, https://doi.org/10.1007/978-1-4842-9169-6_8

*There is no single, simple explanation for what has been hap-
pening in the world. But when you look at it closely you do
find some common threads. Among the most significant to me
is a realization by human beings world-wide that they, as
individuals, deserve to count for something, regardless of
social structure, or, to return to the military analogy, rank. An
equally significant thread that runs through this modern revolution is the power derived through giving freedom of action
to those who seek it. I call these two threads intertwined
together, the "new freedom."*

—*Colonel Mike Wyly*

There is a paradox at the heart of modern management: balancing
management control with creative freedom.

Management controls exist for good reasons—realizing consistent
business profits or standardizing operations for efficiency, for example.
But unchecked management control can throttle innovation. Innovation
requires a type of creative freedom to challenge the operating norms for
discovering and creating new business value.

Therefore, building a great organization that can continuously
innovate requires balancing management control with creative freedom.

If the teams must operate at their creative best, the management has to
learn to become creative with their control.[1]

The management has to know how to read the organizational contexts
to recognize a need for new learning. They have to know when the existing
controls are limiting possible new learning. They have to realize that
someone else's best practice can only be a starting point for their best
possible learning for their organization.

I quoted a description of such creative management from Colonel
Mike Wyly at the beginning. It is a pithy distillation of what modern
management ought to be—less about managerial control, more about
providing this new creative freedom.[2],[3]

This distillation is an imperative for every modern business. And because software is the substrate of so much of new business innovation, it is equally an imperative for the business of software—for software companies and for every enterprise that wants to *become a software company*.

It provides a clarity that is missing from modern management literature. There is an astonishing amount of management literature coming out, with tons of new frameworks to deal with the quickening pace of change in markets and business. There is a bewildering array of new terms for organizing the business enterprise—"learning organizations," "inverted pyramids," "spider plants," "shamrocks," "third-wave organizations," "lean organizations," "cluster organizations," or "virtual enterprises."[4] What should an organization try to model? One of them, all of them? Amid this noise, Colonel Wyly's prescription offers a good reflection on the related management challenge.

For example, you want your teams to self-organize, but without losing their way. You want to innovate, but how can you avoid the legacy incentive of avoiding failure at all costs? You have to keep a long-term focus. Yet, how can you also be accountable for producing short-term results? You have to rely on the emergent value of human teamwork. But how is that possible if you source temporary external teams and developers?

These are not straightforward questions to answer within a large enterprise environment. In my experience of engaging with the highest levels of enterprise software management, they understand the need to organize and manage differently. The *new understanding* for providing this *new freedom* exists. The actual struggle is in finding practical and context-specific *new actions* to deal with the inherent tension of the management paradoxes.[5]

The new actions are often hard to pin down because there isn't a linear relationship between the new understanding and the new action. Within the complexity of modern organizations that run on a web of fast-changing information, the understandings and actions evolve in reference to each other. Mandating top-down new actions doesn't work anymore, because the learning doesn't go in a straight line down the vertical corporate hierarchy. The best learning happens in continuous loops in a self-organized way at every level of the corporate hierarchy.

That's what Colonel Wyly is referring to when he says that the only way the teams have to be set on is in knowing the *way of doing business*. The fundamental responsibility for creative management is to communicate and shape the operating context for teams: market challenges, business opportunities and challenges, changes in strategic directions, and soliciting solutions from the teams as and when the problems arise. And beyond that, mostly stay out of the way.

However, this type of creative management isn't a natural practice within most enterprise software organizations. Most software initiatives start with prioritizing the needs of management control, not the creative aspect of teams building software. Not surprising, because modern management practice is still reeling from effects of a century-long legacy of bureaucratic and mechanistic control.

A Brief Exploration into the Origins of Management Control

No management will self-assess their organization as bureaucratic, even though there are plenty of bureaucratic aspects in all organizations. While there are variations across organizations, an organization can't exist without elements of bureaucracy—division of tasks, hierarchical supervision, and detailed organizational rules and policies. Just as a machine routinizes the process of organizational production, a bureaucracy routinizes the process of organizational administration.[6]

German sociologist Max Weber defined bureaucracy, the first one to define it so, rather favorably:

*a form of organization that emphasizes precision,
speed, clarity, regularity, reliability, and efficiency
achieved through the creation of a fixed division of
tasks, hierarchical supervision, and detailed rules
and regulation.*

Wait a second. What? Don't we understand bureaucracy to be an organization that possesses qualities that are precisely the opposite of the ones Weber is listing? Where did the meaning change?

It changed a little bit after Weber said this. And we can blame scientific management theorists who fell in love with the pursuit of efficiency. Weber had advocated caution. He had warned that the bureaucratic approach could erode the human spirit and capacity for spontaneous action. But the management theorists only focused on only defining management principles for achieving the best bureaucratization, setting aside the concerns Weber had expressed.

Scientific management, headlined by Frederick Winslow Taylor's work, focused on maximizing production efficiency. Taylor had a famous collaboration with Henry Ford at the beginning of the twentieth century. They transformed the assembly process of the vehicle. Instead of skilled mechanics assembling the car start to finish, the vehicle was moved along an assembly line. The various workers stationed alongside the line did one small and straightforward assembly task. With that, the production time came down from 12 hours to 93 minutes, and the price came down from $825 to $575.[7] And as they say, the rest is history.

This concept of assembly line took off and became an embodiment of mass-producing a template good. It wasn't just due to Taylor and management theorists of his ilk pushing it. The industrial world of the early and mid-twentieth century, driven by constraints of wars, pulled hard at it. The resulting effect has been bittersweet. It accelerated industrial productivity, but hastened the replacement of skilled craftsmanship with unskilled workers. All the increases in productivity came at a human cost, reducing a large proportion of workers into automatons.

Though not intentional, Taylor ended up creating this duality between management and workers with his approach. Management was an entity that defined the what and how of the tasks of workers. His original principles weren't all that detrimental to the worker agency in favor of strengthening management control. But when these principles were sought by management and applied in management interest, they ended up achieving the effect of eliminating the worker agency—exactly as Weber had portended.

The influence of Taylor's approach has been summarized well by Gareth Morgan in his book *Images of Organization*[8]:

> *The principles advocated by Taylor and perfected by McDonald's and other fast-food restaurants have found their way into the organization of hospitals, factories, retail outlets, schools, universities, and other institutions seeking to rationalize their operations.*

When all the enterprise businesses that Morgan is referring to started digitizing and digitalizing their operations with IT and software, the same production approach made its way into technology and software management as well.

Today, the responsibility to organize enterprise software development into a detailed project plan resides largely with managers. For the developers, eventually, each development task is defined in a highly precise way as a development ticket for a developer to complete (referred to as a user story) just like an assembly line task.[1] Doing work means completing your user story tickets. These tickets are highly truncated stories, such that developers have very little understanding of what the enterprise business is doing.

---

[1] David Heinemeier Hansson, CTO of Basecamp, refers to commonly used JIRA-type backlog management as "ticket treadmills."

So depending on whom you ask, the lived experience of a modern enterprise software practitioner may not be too different from that of an assembly line worker in the Taylor-Ford era. We are making knowledge goods with a mindset of making physical goods. While the industrial era may be far back in the rearview mirror, the legacy of it lives on.

Mechanistic to Organic: The Evolving Nature of Management Control

The ideal worker for an assembly line was "someone with limited imagination, boundless patience, and a willingness to obediently do the same repetitive tasks day in and out."[7] It needs no arguing that this worker archetype is the least desirable in modern organizations, software development or otherwise.

You require an archetype that is a complete opposite, at least in theory. They may not be allowed to exercise it every day, but a modern employee is expected to leverage their full imagination at work. They are expected to not be patient with the status quo, but actually required to lead and drive change. Ones considered innovative are those who bring ideas to automate the daily, repetitive tasks.

While an assembly line worker had to be amenable to mechanistic control, an ideal modern employee is expected to contribute a new type of bottom-up control, organic control, to stay vigilant and ward off the ill effects of ever-encroaching bureaucracy within an organization. This is a result of a century-long evolution of organizing a business enterprise in response to the changing pace of market environments.

Table 8-1. *Evolution of Management Control from Mechanistic to Organic (Source: Images of Organization)*

	Mechanistic Control	**Organic Control**
Nature of external environment	Relatively stable.	Unpredictable/turbulent.
Nature of business opportunity	Mass-produce a template product efficiently.	Explore and exploit new market situations by innovating on rapid technological change.
Organization of work	Clear and narrowly defined jobs arranged within a well-defined hierarchy.	Avoid specifying individual tasks; employees define jobs in interaction with an immediate leader and peers.
Nature of authority	Well-defined and vested in formal positions within the hierarchy.	Informal and changing and vested in teams and individuals with appropriate skills and abilities.
Communication patterns	As per the rules and policies, vertical, up and down the hierarchy.	Free and informal; constraining communication can be rate limiting to what an organization can do (Conway's Law).
Nature of employee commitment	To the responsibilities associated with the job, loyalty, and obedience.	To the overall purpose of the organization; requires an ability to deal with stress and uncertainty.

This differentiation between mechanistic and organic control was first highlighted by two British researchers, Burns and Stalker, in 1961.[2] They compared a rayon manufacturer (requiring mechanistic control) and an electronics manufacturer (requiring organic control) as the two extremes.

If the pace of change was deemed turbulent for an electronics company in the Burns-Stalker analysis, think about what it would be for a modern software company. The pace of change for a software company can only be described as seismic. An electronics firm of that era needed to update their products one to two times per year. A software company, depending on the market it is in, is expected to update its products or services daily. The pace of change may be not as torrid for an enterprise company becoming a software company. But even then, the expectation for them to update products and services could be at least three to four times per year.

As compared with today, try to recall those yearly Microsoft Windows updates of the late 1990s. It felt like a great pace of change at that time, but now seems like a glacial one. The concept of shipping "good enough" software that Microsoft pioneered has been put on steroids.[9] The modern cloud and mobile platforms have completely changed the paradigm. Software, in our hands or in general, is subject to constant change now, either to satisfy new uses or when it outgrows the hardware. The fast-changing technologies in turn shape the changing aspirations of customers and marketplaces. As a result, the customer and market problems also evolve faster than ever in response.

Understanding and solving a customer problem is not a discrete planning event anymore. To deal with the flux of customer aspirations and adjusting marketplaces, it must be a constant iterative process. The amount of information processing at an organization level can't

---

[2] Gareth Morgan provides a more modern analysis in his 1986 book *Images of Organization.*

be managed with mechanistic and bureaucratic control. Organizations have to rely on self-organizing at the level of development teams and individuals within those teams.

Organic control is foundational to self-organizing teams and self-learning organizations. That is the enduring insight of the Burns and Stalker analysis. While some level of mechanistic control will always stay as an entrenched artifact, every new ecology of organizations in every new group of industries since has been evolving the idea of organic control in response to the flux of changing environments.

In the Burns-Stalker analysis, a rayon firm, a switch-gear firm, a radio and television firm, and an electronics firm were representatives of the new ecologies within the flux. I am adding a software firm as a representative of the newest ecology of firms. The Age of Software has turbocharged the flux. What we know from studying those firms is that a software firm can't innovate without organic control. In fact, if an enterprise wants to become a software firm, it needs an accelerated evolution toward organic control.

Paradoxes, Contexts, and Attractors

Organic control is a brilliant concept because it encapsulates the required balance between control and freedom. It is a right term to shed the naive idealism of allowing creative work that seems impractical for large enterprises. It creates the right focus on dealing with the paradoxes of business change.

Related to this, I am reminded of a story I heard from an enterprise software practitioner at a conference a few years ago. About his role, he told me, "I push a button to run a software job. If something goes wrong, I report a defect for an external team to fix. Otherwise, when the job completes, I send an email and wait for next week's run." He was obviously exaggerating to describe the lack of agency in his day job. His example may be describing an extreme case of a person straight-jacketed with mechanistic control.

I have observed and interacted with hundreds of enterprise software people in their roles. A vast majority of enterprise software roles require being imaginative. Also, people have plenty of choices to change their jobs as compared with an assembly line worker of the early twentieth century. Moreover, the pace of technological change ensures that tasks to be done change often.

Therefore, an average case of today's enterprise software practitioner is a dilemma. They understand that the changing business environments require them to adopt new behaviors, *new actions*. They understand the forks in the road—the need to move away from old actions toward new actions. But they get stymied when the management doesn't deal with the paradox of the expected changes adequately.

We started with a general paradox—providing creative freedom without causing confusion or chaos. Let us understand it more. A practitioner deals with many such paradoxes (as represented in Table 8-2).

Table 8-2. *The Paradoxes of Enterprise Technology Management (Adapted from Images of Organization)*

New Behavior Pattern Required	Old Dominant Behavior Pattern
Innovate with new technologies.	Avoid implementation mistakes.
Long-term/strategic focus.	Deliver short-term results.
Improve motivation/morale.	Cut technology spend.
Improve teamwork.	Reduce in-house staff/teams.
Flexible to change.	Follow detailed IT policies.
Collaborate with technology partners.	Account for competitive concerns.
Provide decision-making freedom.	Avoid chaos and confusion.
Specialize and differentiate.	Own the technology stack.
Deliver high quality.	Keep the costs low.

The business change in enterprise environment is difficult due to the tension that builds within these paradoxes. For example, you don't just need innovation. You must maximize innovation while minimizing mistakes. Every technology investment starts with a long-term vision, yet the solution delivery expectations are short term. There is never infinite time to achieve a product-market or solution-customer fit. The expectation is to do more with less. An added expectation is to maintain the employee morale even though technology spend shrinks.

The large business change and technology transformation programs are almost always staffed with temporary external teams. And teamwork is the first casualty in temporary organizational structures. But working with an external team is an existential reality.

The increasing complexity of technology stacks necessitates partnering, but the collaboration may have a competitive tension. The work has to be high quality, compliant with regulations, but it has to be done at the lowest cost possible.

The change management gets complex because the management typically pushes only one half of the paradox. If the teams perceive the new behavior pattern more attractive, the change becomes easier. But when the teams perceive the expectations of new behaviors unreasonable, because the operating norms make old behavior attractive, they revert to old behaviors.

This is where management of organizational context, what side of the paradox should be more attractive, becomes critical. In short, just the management expectations of their teams won't yield the desired business change. The management has to work to shape attractors through shaping organizational operating context. Within an enterprise that is a mature business, both sides of the paradox are worthy of attention. The management can't focus on just breaking the resistance to change, an element of mechanistic control. They also have to shape the attractors for new actions, an element of organic control. Like we learned in the Team Principle, it is "Team=Software" philosophy in action. The management has to model what they expect from their teams first, for the teams to follow.

Consider the *minimum spec* principle we encountered in the discussion of the Value Principle. If you assign a business problem, instead of a predetermined solution to deliver, with guardrails being the specific mistakes to avoid, you are creating a context that is an attractor for innovation. A long list of requirements to be done within a fixed time and budget creates a context that is an attractor for avoiding mistakes.

Another huge context-shaping lever is investing in processes and infrastructure that maximize development flow.[3] Are the teams equipped to work in small batches to produce short-term results? Are they empowered to constrain the work in process (WIP) to manage the long-term focus? Is there good continuous integration and deployment infrastructure to make cadence delivery possible in a compliant way?

Another such lever is making deliberate RBRB (rent, buy, reuse, build) micro-decisions for creating a dynamic software stack that *minimizes*

---

[3] The Flow Principle, Chapter 6.

the work to be not done.[4] That helps in managing the dilemma of how to collaborate with partners while differentiating and owning the mission-critical pieces of the stack. Similarly, insourcing teams, instead of outsourcing work, can help in emphasizing teamwork while addressing the desire to keep costs manageable.[5]

These examples are management actions aligned with organic control—management's reciprocal obligation for making their teams Agile. The management delivering on these actions changes the prevailing contexts and attractors for software teams. When management takes these actions, as a quid pro quo, they make the new actions of the paradox attractive for the entire organization.[5] With these actions, the teams can see the *need* for the change. It strengthens their *belief* that they can fulfill the need, with the support of their management. They see fulfilling the need as an *opportunity* to learn new things and advance their careers. With these actions, the management and the teams share the *anticipation* of a better future for their internal and external customers. When individuals can experience these attractors—*need, belief, opportunity*, and *anticipation*—within the context of their work, the work becomes meaningful.[1]

Meaningful work is the ultimate attractor for building teams geared to innovate. Yet, despite enterprises knowing the benefits of engaging employees through meaningful work, they find it hard to get it right consistently. I call it the case of attractor confusion. When the teams are gelling, their work output has a good market fit, and it is resulting in good business outcomes,-all organizations tout the meaningfulness of the work they offer and how organically they operate. However, when the going gets tough due to the down business cycle or changing market conditions, they revert back to mechanistic control.

Just when they should be putting more attention into reading paradoxes and prevailing operating contexts and adjusting attractors, they do the reverse.

---

[4] The Stack Principle, Chapter 4.
[5] The Team Principle, Chapter 7.

The Case of Attractor Confusion

We can blame McKinsey & Company for attractor confusion. They published a highly influential quarterly briefing titled "The War for Talent" in 1998.[10] The War for Talent is credited with starting the transformation of human resources departments "from dull administrative service providers into bells-and-whistles, make-or-break, core corporate functions that merited seats at the top table."[11] Apart from introducing the word *talent* to the corporate lexicon, the briefing and the book that followed normalized the notion that just prioritizing great talent is all you need to build a great organization.

The McKinsey paper was wildly popular, but there were some critical voices. The most notable of those voices was of author Malcolm Gladwell. In 2002, Gladwell published an analysis in the *New Yorker* called "The Talent Myth."[12]

Gladwell made Enron the central case study for his analysis. He wrote about Enron:

> *It was a company where McKinsey conducted twenty*
> *separate projects, where McKinsey's billings topped*
> *ten million dollars a year, where a McKinsey director*
> *regularly attended board meetings, and where the*
> *C.E.O. himself was a former McKinsey partner.*

Enron had followed McKinsey's prescription quite literally. It was the "ultimate talent company." But it had to file for bankruptcy in 2001 with its top two executives, Jeff Skilling and Kenneth Lay, prison bound.

There is no doubt that talented individuals are required for successful organizations in the age of knowledge work. But the research shows that great teams outperform the collection of more talented individuals every day.[13] We can observe that prominently in professional sports. The teams with superstars paid the highest salaries don't always win against the more effective teams. It isn't true in just sports. Any work that requires individuals to work effectively in groups is keyed on effective collaboration—free and informal as required for organic control.

New software-based intellectual property development is a prime example of such group work. It isn't surprising that collaboration is the key to creating repeatable and predictable new value with software as well.[14]

While great talent is necessary, it doesn't guarantee a great organization. What matters more than the individual ability is the *system* in which the individual operates. What does *system* refer to here? Culture, organizational structure, and the way the management shapes the operating context through attractors, and communicates within and across that structure—in short, the organization itself. Therefore, it isn't the good individual talent that makes organizations smart. It is the other way around—it is the quality of the organization that makes the good talent great.[12]

Enron had the best talent, but the system in which that talent operated paved the way for a bankruptcy. Over-indexing on individual talent and ignoring the system of collaborative teamwork can be hazardous to the organization.

Enron's is a cautionary tale of enacting the individual "talent mindset" advocated by McKinsey taken to its extreme. Even though no organization recruits, hires, or rewards the talent like Enron did, the legacy of the talent mindset lingers in the HR departments. Higher individual bonuses for top performers, relative performance ratings where individuals are pitted against each other, and various other individual financial performance incentives were born out of the ethos of the talent mindset. That is the state of the art of managing talent within the modern firms—software or otherwise. Organizations rewarding individuals over teams are the direct legacy of the talent mindset.

I have written self-assessments for my performance. I sit on the review panels where the performance of others is reviewed. While considerable work has been done to expand the assessments beyond individual performance, including the quality of collaborative work, the final set of decisions still involve sifting individuals to put them in various buckets for individual rewards. The ultimate decisions still favor high-quality individuals over high-quality collaborative work.

I am not arguing that management and organizations should stop rewarding talented individuals. Instead, what I am saying is that until the management deliberately nurtures the system for collaborative teamwork, they shouldn't expect innovative software-based intellectual property.

Trust Your Teams to Deliver on Their Mission

The labor upheavals of the COVID-19 pandemic provide an insight on how attracting talent with financial rewards isn't enough. First, there was the trend called the Great Resignation, when employees quit their jobs at higher-than-usual rates.[15] It was followed by the Quiet Quitting, where the surveys reported the employees do the minimum work necessary to keep their job.[16] These two trends have been interpreted in many ways, but one thing is incontrovertible. The modern firms struggle to meaningfully engage their employees through right attractors.

The Great Resignation and Quiet Quitting happened despite the firms shelling absurd amounts of money to recruit and retain talent. Money didn't work because these two trends are outcomes of the case of attractor confusion. Although they get analyzed in terms of the employees, they say more about the management. They put a spotlight on the management's inability to get the attractors right.

When the pandemic eased, organizations resorted to tactics that can be classified as mechanistic control—mandatory return to work (RTO) policies that provoke voluntary attrition, forcing in-office work after hiring people with a promise of remote work. Here, even the firms like Amazon, which can be counted as successes of the software age, aren't immune.

After empowering teams to decide how they work, they are mandating three times a week in the office—a policy hostile to employees recruited with a promise of remote work.[17]

At the core of this tussle, happening very widely, is the lack of trust between management and staff. The nature of authority enacted by management reflects alignment with mechanistic control. The perceived causality for low productivity is presumed to be remote work. But what if the actual reason is lack of employee engagement? But what if the lack of meaningful work is the real cause of low engagement?

Jim and Michele McCarthy note in their book that the central issue for increasing collaboration is "surmounting distance." But they are quick to clarify that while physical distance matters, what matters more is the "psychological distance."[18] I am not questioning the efficacy of in-person face-to-face collaboration here. What I am questioning is the lack of trust shown in the teams to self-organize by the companies mandating RTO. Maybe if the teams were entrusted with self-organizing, that is, the task to determine the co-locating plan required to fulfill their mission, they might have come up with some combination of in-person and remote themselves.

My teams have been remote first even before COVID. We always allow our teams to self-organize (and co-locate) as required by them to execute their roles. We focus on reducing the psychological distance while teams figure out how to manage the physical distance.

With self-organization, the management has to trust the emergent outcomes of the interactions with teams and individuals, over some predetermined and short-term outcomes. This is what Colonel Wyly meant when he referred to people sharing "a code of honor" that binds them in mutual trust. The people here mean both management and team. Without trust, there can be no self-organizing that is critical for modern organizations.

Self-Organization Is Mandatory for Agile Decision Making

Genghis is a mobile robot (a mo-bot) that was created at MIT. Kevin Kelly, founder of *Wired* magazine, has described it as a "mechanical cockroach." Each leg of this robotic cockroach has a microprocessor and sensing devices to "think" and "determine" each leg's action. The central control is merely a set of simple rules for sequences for lifting legs. The walking action emerges from the leg lifting rules acting on sensory intelligence of each leg.[19]

This design eliminates the problem of centralized processing of sensing information from each leg and coordinating operations of all legs, referred to as "the body problem" within the field. The body problem happens when a large centralized computer (*brain*) requires so much supporting hardware (*body*) that it gets immobilized due to the large body to brain ratio. Genghis, instead, relies on a decentralized and a bottom-up intelligence, which emerges from the interaction of *thinking* local agents operating under simple behavioral rules.[19]

Genghis is a great metaphor for understanding the challenge of self-organization: *avoiding the body problem.* A highly centralized decision making results in a body problem for an organization. If the teams aren't innovating or they are taking too long to deliver, your organization may have a body problem: centralized control with too few thinking local agents.

The level of sensory information for an organization due to the fast-changing markets and fast-changing customer constraints is so immense that you need information processing within your executing teams to avoid the body problem.

Let's review the following example. A manufacturer *based* in the United States can coordinate assembly of the final product in China or Vietnam from parts manufactured in nearby factories. It can further coordinate deliveries of the finished product in various global markets. The customer helplines can be operated from anywhere. The US-based organization typically owns the marketing and research functions. All that is possible because modern organizations rest on and run from a web of information.[20]

Similarly, software has transformed the process of software development. The collaboration and DevOps tools have converted software development into an information processing activity. The rough ideas are developed and managed as information wikis in a tool like Confluence. Once fully researched, they are recorded as user stories and organized in *sprints of work* in a tool like Jira. The code is developed and stored in repositories within code management tools like Bitbucket, including configuration files to automate the installation and deployment. There are continuous deployment and integration tools like Jenkins and Bamboo to build, test, and deploy code changes into system environments. Each developer focuses on a small piece of this entire puzzle. Organizations develop software from all the activities that rest on and run from a web of information housed within these tools.

With this complex web of information, the source of innovation is the self-organizing team, like a leg of Genghis. Customer needs and requirements aren't the source of innovative ideas. They are the starting point. The actual source is the ideas to remove the incongruities that are preventing the customer from making progress.[6] The customers don't know what is possible with software. The innovations comes from the solutions that self-organizing teams create who understand the customer's problem deeply.

The translation of ideas to innovative solutions is primarily an information processing problem. Therefore, the primary question for an

---

[6] The Value Principle, Chapter 2.

organization that wants to be a learning organization is: how efficient is the information flow to, within, and across self-organizing teams as the new ideas are converted to working software?[7]

The reason the org charts can be such a limiting factor for what organizations can ship revolves around what it does to the information flow. An org chart often mainly represents the vertical hierarchy for decision making—an element of importance for mechanistic control. But organic control can't result from organizational thinking that happens up and down the vertical hierarchy. It results from the continuous thinking that happens within various information loops that exist within the organization at all levels. Organic control is an emergent outcome within organizations that adopt and act on learning happening at all levels of hierarchy.

Continuous Learning and Embracing Emergent Outcomes

Each business enterprise has an identity—a carmaker, drugmaker, online search provider, or consultancy. When that enterprise analyzes its operating market environment, its understanding is a product of its identity. This understanding isn't embedded in some standalone external reference of the market. The understanding is self-referential. Business innovation is hard because the flux in the external environment outpaces the rate at which the enterprise can change its identity.[21]

Although there is a distinction between the identity and environment, they evolve together as an interconnected pattern. A desire of a carmaker to become a software company is pulled upon by the imperative for software companies to navigate the business change. But can the new identity of a carmaker evolve from understanding how to build

---

[7] The Flow Principle, Chapter 6.

software? Because their understanding of software development will be self-referential, they will tend to look at producing software with an understanding of how they produce cars. We saw the evidence of this confusion when we reviewed the complexity of building software and the struggle of carmakers at software.[8]

Their new understanding of the need to become a software company is enough to get started. It highlights the direction in which it needs to go. But what will get them there? A new action for continuous learning from building and shipping software.[5] That was a point of differentiation between traditional carmakers and Tesla. Tesla was organized to ship software with a car, while traditional carmakers were organized to ship a car with software. The traditional carmakers' new understanding of their identity is a starting point for their new actions. Their learning from new actions should inform their new understanding and vice versa. This must happen in a continuous loop, where they adjust their operating norms from their learnings from each loop. They don't need to copy what Tesla is doing. They have to rely on this loop between new understanding and new action. Their new identity will emerge over time and will be differentiated from Tesla's.

Similarly, Agile software development is an emergent outcome of learning in loops. It is impossible in enterprises that have institutionalized a single loop learning. *We know Agile works. Let us implement Scrum, and everything will be fine.* It happens only within enterprises that institutionalize learning through continuous loops. *Let us build Agile culture and evolve through continuous learning of the flow principles as it makes sense for our organization.* Furthermore, it happens only in enterprises that trust the interconnected and evolutionary pattern of new understandings and new actions. It happens only in enterprises that embrace the emergence of new actions over dictating new actions. A real learning organization emerges from thousands of continuous interactions between the management and the teams.

---

[8] The Complexity Principle, Chapter 3.

The Art of Creative Management

Creating new business value with software requires creative work. Organizing such software development work requires creative management.

Creative management has very little to do with managing people. It has a lot to do with creating a system to make the people effective. It is about creating a mission-oriented culture that prioritizes mutual trust and intuitive knowledge as values and is focused on a strategy to win in the marketplace. Not only that, it is about creating an organizational structure that maximizes information flow to maximize the process of building value. It is about entrusting small and self-organized teams in such a culture and a structure to realize value, instead of asking resources to deliver work on a negotiated spec.

Creative management is about providing creative freedom without causing confusion—by redefining management control, addressing business change management as a contextual problem, and embracing continuous improvement and learning as a way of operating.

1. *Increasing Organic Control, Reducing Mechanistic Control*

    Most functions of administering a modern organization have already been automated by software. The differentiation comes from exploring and exploiting new market opportunities: inventing new business models, reducing friction in the internal and external customer experience, and operational excellence with software.

    The opportunity isn't in merely implementing newer technologies. The real opportunity lies in inventing new ways of doing business, differentiated and unique to each business enterprise. That requires creativity that can only come for a type of *new freedom*: a decision-making discretion for workers, employees, and developers.

The management has to achieve a right balance between mechanistic control and organic control—more organic, less mechanistic. This balance isn't required just to reduce the human cost of too much bureaucratic control. It is required because this balance is critical for enterprises trying to succeed in the fast-paced business environments in the Age of Software.

2. *Reading Contexts for Business Change and Adjusting Relevant Attractors*

    Addressing management paradoxes and adjusting context to create attractors for your talent aren't proficiencies for most organizations. They are good at staying "on course." Sensing the market, setting new business objectives, and monitoring performance against those objectives are the elements of basic management competency that is institutionalized.

    What isn't institutionalized is reading and adjusting operating contexts for the required business change. Are the managers and executives trained to manage the paradoxes inherent in business change? Do the people executing the change have the agency to adjust the operating norms? Can the software teams and individuals change course if an old attractor is preventing them from making progress?

    You may think you have created empowered teams. But have you done enough to offset the old hierarchy's pull to retain control?

    There will always be an inherent tension with business change management. But are you treating that as a political problem? That is, are you focused on managing resistance to change and engaging in corporate politics? Or are you treating that as a challenge to create new business attractors for effecting the required change?

3. *Embracing Continuous Improvement and Learning*

This is perhaps the hardest aspect of creative management. Most managers aren't trained in complexity theory and managing systems as a whole. The art of corporate management is commonly understood as managing budgets, allocating resources, and avoiding mistakes. Assigning responsibility as a two-way contract, trusting teams to deliver on the assigned missions, and learning from emerging outcomes as they happen have a level of uncertainty that the corporate world needs to embrace.

David Heinemeier Hansen describes the art of modern management as creating and "getting out of the momentum's way"[22]:

It can take a long time and be tricky business to get a gaggle of humans rolling in the same, right direction. When it finally happens, you feel it. The pace is effortless. The interactions are easy. This is the moment when momentum asks you to get out of the way. The easiest way to mess up a good thing is to mess with it at all. Just leave it alone and marvel at the magic!

Good reading of the context means recognizing the momentum, or lack thereof. Even if it isn't there, it doesn't mean jumping to micromanage. It should mean adjusting the operating norms and letting the outcomes emerge, instead of forcing them. New actions don't result from new understandings in a one-time transformation, but they feed on each other in a continuous loop. That is why a one-time big transformation is a wrong metaphor for implementing business change. The right metaphor is continuous improvement and embracing learning as a way of operating.

The Management Principle   Practice the art of creative management. Create bottom-up organic control, manage organizational operating contexts to make change attractive, and embrace continuous learning.

Key Tenets:

- Building a great organization that can continuously innovate requires balancing management control with creative freedom. In the Age of Software, this is also the central management challenge for becoming a software company.

- This is hard for enterprise companies because they are used to exercising mechanistic control in pursuit of efficient production and standardizing operations.

- Mechanistic management control is a legacy of Taylor's scientific management and a widespread success of efficient production with an assembly line approach.

- But when creating innovation with software, the management needs to build up a bottom-up organic control. With the pace of change in market problems and required solutions, organic control vested with small teams is the only approach that works.

- That means managing paradoxes of change that involve tension between legacy behavior patterns and new required behavior patterns, that is, new actions. Organic control requires that management focuses on making new actions attractive, instead of breaking resistance to change.

- Management should shape attractors for new actions by taking actions that change the context of existing operations. They should make new actions organically attractive over old actions.

- Management should be aware of the problem of attractor confusion. The top attractor isn't money, but meaningful work. Communicating clear missions and allowing teams to self-organize make the work meaningful.

- Self-organization is mandatory for Agile decision making. It requires embracing continuous learning and knowing that new understandings of their operating context and new actions evolve as an interconnected pattern.

- Creating new business value with software requires creative work. Organizing such software development work requires creative management. The following are the key ideas for practicing creative management:

- Increasing bottom-up organic control, reducing top-down mechanistic control

- Managing contexts for business change and adjusting relevant attractors to make new actions attractive

- Embracing continuous improvement and learning as a way of operating

References

[1] Bond, G. (2020, June 17). *Why are CEOs failing software engineers.* iiSM.org. Retrieved September 15, 2020, from `https://iism.org/article/why-are-ceos-failing-software-engineers-56`

[2] Richards, C. (2004). *Certain to Win: The Strategy of John Boyd, Applied to Business* (Kindle ed., page 108). Xlibris.

[3] Wyly, M. D. (1991). *Thinking Like Marines.* Slightly East of New. Retrieved April 15, 2023, from `https://slightlyeastofnew.com/2012/03/21/thinking-like-marines/`

[4] Morgan, G. (2006). *Images of Organization* (updated ed., page 52). SAGE Publications.

[5] Morgan, G. (2006). Images of Organization (updated ed., page 270). SAGE Publications.

[6] Morgan, G. (2006). *Images of Organization* (updated ed., page 17). SAGE Publications.

[7] Suzman, J. (2021). *Work: A Deep History, from the Stone Age to the Age of Robots* (Kindle ed., page 332). Penguin Publishing Group.

[8] Morgan, G. (2006). *Images of Organization* (updated ed., page 24). SAGE Publications.

[9] Wilson, M. (2009, April 27). *The New Mantra of Tech: It's Good Enough.* Gizmodo. Retrieved April 15, 2023, from `https://gizmodo.com/the-new-mantra-of-tech-its-good-enough-5229951`

[10] Chambers, E. G., Foulon, M., Handfield-Jones, H., & Hankin, S. M. (January 1998). *The War for Talent*. McKinsey Quarterly. www.researchgate.net/publication/284689712_The_War_for_Talent

[11] Suzman, J. (2021). *Work: A Deep History, from the Stone Age to the Age of Robots* (Kindle ed., page 354). Penguin Publishing Group.

[12] Gladwell, M. (2002, July 14). *The Talent Myth*. The New Yorker. Retrieved April 15, 2023, from www.newyorker.com/magazine/2002/07/22/the-talent-myth

[13] Pfeffer, J. (2001). *Fighting the War for Talent Is Hazardous to Your Organization's Health*. Stanford Graduate School of Business. Retrieved April 17, 2023, from www.gsb.stanford.edu/faculty-research/working-papers/fighting-war-talent-hazardous-your-organizations-health

[14] McCarthy, J., & McCarthy, M. (2002). *Software for Your Head: Core Protocols for Creating and Maintaining Shared Vision* (page 167). Addison-Wesley.

[15] *Great Resignation*. (n.d.). Wikipedia. Retrieved April 15, 2023, from https://en.wikipedia.org/wiki/Great_Resignation

[16] Zenger, J., & Folkman, J. (2022, August 31). *Quiet Quitting Is About Bad Bosses, Not Bad Employees*. Harvard Business Review. Retrieved April 15, 2023, from https://hbr.org/2022/08/quiet-quitting-is-about-bad-bosses-not-bad-employees

[17] Orosz, G. (2023, February 24). *Tweet*. https://twitter.com/GergelyOrosz. Retrieved April 17, 2023, from https://twitter.com/GergelyOrosz/status/1629159189011484673?s=20

[18]   McCarthy, J., & McCarthy, M. (2002). *Software for Your Head: Core Protocols for Creating and Maintaining Shared Vision* (page 167). Addison-Wesley.

[19]   Morgan, G. (2006). *Images of Organization* (updated ed., page 77). SAGE Publications.

[20]   Morgan, G. (2006). *Images of Organization* (updated ed., page 81). SAGE Publications.

[21]   Morgan, G. (2006). *Images of Organization* (updated ed., page 259). SAGE Publications.

[22]   Hansson, D. H. (2023, February 24). *Get out of momentum's way*. HEY. Retrieved April 15, 2023, from `https://world.hey.com/dhh/get-out-of-momentum-s-way-765248d2`

Conclusion

No man ever steps in the same river twice, for it is not the same river and he is not the same man.

—Heraclitus

I started writing this book with the quest to answer one question: *How to become a software company?* I had a notion of an answer, an outline. I would call it a blurry image of the final picture, at best. Brush by brush, the picture came together. Word by word, the answer and the book came together.

Writing this book was hard and humbling work. Initially, I tried to complete writing on a fixed plan, but struggled mightily. I was fast approaching my estimated deadline, but getting nowhere. I had to make a mental shift. I stopped worrying about the deadline, but more about writing the best book I could.

I recommitted to the process of writing on a cadence—show up for writing 30–45 minutes every day and move it a little bit forward every day. With each day, it became obvious to me that what I really wanted to say was best discovered in the process of writing itself. It is impossible to think it through in your head.

After finishing this book, it is my firm personal belief that creativity is an emergent outcome of doing, not thinking or planning. For every chapter and the book, I ended up creating something different and better from what I originally intended. The final picture for each chapter and the book emerged through a process of iterative discovery and refinement.

A. Sidhu, *Becoming a Software Company*, https://doi.org/10.1007/978-1-4842-9169-6

In that sense, writing this book became a good metaphor for the principles I am outlining in this book for building and managing software for new and differentiated enterprise business value.

Innovative software that creates new and differentiated business can't come from executing elaborate plans. It comes from iterative learning by doing while serving the interest of creating progress for your customers.

So how can an enterprise become a software company?

By continuously improving at creating repeatable and predictable business value with software.

Becoming a software company requires making the enterprise software development and management a creative exercise.

It is about leveraging software as a medium of producing new value as described in the following principles:

1. **The Shift Principle**: Don't pursue large and wasteful digital transformations. Instead, continuously improve at building and shipping software. Make your software shift.

2. **The Value Principle**: Create new value through customer (internal and external) progress. Don't just gather and meet business requirements with new and newer technologies at the lowest possible cost.

3. **The Complexity Principle**: Software can generate seemingly limitless value, but it is complex to get it right. Always look to minimize the system complexity to multiply value from your software investments.

   It is about optimizing your technology foundation, organizational culture, and development processes to leverage the agility of software as a medium of producing value as described in the following principles:

4. **The Stack Principle**: Don't procure software through traditional buy or build analyses. Create a dynamic and differentiated software stack that minimizes the amount of development work. A dynamic stack is the foundation of agility.

5. **The Culture Principle**: Agile software development happens only in an Agile business environment. Therefore, implement your strategy of business agility before you implement Agile development methods.

6. **The Flow Principle**: Don't fixate on managing project or product timelines and budgets. Instead, focus on managing the software development flow.

   Subscribing to the preceding principles will make your enterprise a good software company. To become a great software company, you have to rely on your people.

   Don't micromanage your human talent. Trust them to take you from good to great, as explained in the following principles:

7. **The Team Principle**: Build teams. Don't just hire resources, because teams build good software, not a collection of resources.

8. **The Management Principle**: Practice the art of creative management. Create bottom-up organic control, manage operating contexts to make change attractive, and embrace continuous learning.

To become a software company, an enterprise must not violate these principles, at a minimum. At best, these principles should be embedded within the values an enterprise abides by.

CONCLUSION

There are plenty of methods and tactics behind these principles. I deliberately avoided a discussion of those methods to put a spotlight on the underlying principles within this book, because if an enterprise gets these principles right, the methods are just the details. In fact, if the management gets the principles right, the teams will figure out the methodological details.

Understanding and subscribing to these principles helped me with the *becoming a software company transition* within my work. I hope it helps you and your enterprise as well.

Index

© Amarinder Sidhu 2023
A. Sidhu, *Becoming a Software Company*, https://doi.org/10.1007/978-1-4842-9169-6

Printed in the United States
by Baker & Taylor Publisher Services